CHRIST
AND
PROMETHEUS

CHRIST
and
PROMETHEUS

A New Image of the Secular

WILLIAM F. LYNCH, S.J.

UNIVERSITY OF NOTRE DAME PRESS

Library of Congress Catalog Card Number: 70-122046
Manufactured in the United States of America by
NAPCO Graphic Arts, Inc., Milwaukee, Wisconsin

Acknowledgments

Grateful acknowledgment is made for permission to reprint excerpts from the following works:

The plays of Aeschylus as translated by Richmond Lattimore and David Grene in *Aeschylus I* and *Aeschylus II*, published by the University of Chicago Press, 1953 and 1956 respectively. *Oresteia* © 1953 by The University of Chicago. *Prometheus Bound* © 1942 by The University of Chicago.

Archetypal Images in Greek Religion: Vol. 1, *Prometheus* by C. Kerényi, translated by Ralph Manheim, Bollingen Series LXV.1. Copyright © 1963 by the Bollingen Foundation. Reprinted by permission of Princeton University Press.

From pp. 1–2, 4, 7, 27 in *Dynamics of Modernization* by C. E. Black. Copyright © 1966 by C. E. Black. Reprinted by permission of Harper & Row, Publishers, Inc.

Foreword

To remember thanks is also to forget, for it is impossible to remember all the good that was done to me and for me as I wrote this book. First of all there are President John H. Morey and Dean Philip Secor of Muhlenberg College, who made generously sure that a good part of my work as Trexler visiting professor would be the finishing of *Christ and Prometheus*. I therefore also acknowledge a happy debt to the Trexler Foundation.

Work I have done in the past has always had editors who were skillful helpers and good friends. That experience has been a constant good fortune and blessing. Now I wish to thank Ann Rice for the unending patience and competence of her help with this manuscript. Then there is my friend John Golden, S. J., who saved the book from many errors by reading it many times. All fault remaining is mine.

As for myself, looking back at the whole course of the task of writing a book, I would be most thankful if it should make any contribution at all to healing the wounds in the divided imagination of this country at this time and building for it some common vision. Surely that is our terrible need.

Contents

PROLOGUE

I

A Central Metaphor

The Age of Orestes

It is because the genius of Aeschylus is able to direct our thoughts to the constant dramatic process by which human civilization moves through pain toward higher moments of achievement and some verge of innocence that I will be able to use his images and actors as metaphors in this modern study of the secular project.

I shall have much to say of his Prometheus. For it is clear that he is described as legendary initiator of human culture and as sufferer because of it. He is finally reconciled with Zeus, in such a reconciliation with himself and the world as we ourselves, more than we think, still long for. There is in fact a pattern of the search for reconciliation in the whole Aeschylean corpus; this would have emerged with even more clarity if we possessed the plays that were companion to Prometheus Bound and The Suppliant Maidens. However, we do have as incomparable masterpiece the trilogy of the Oresteia, in whose powerful pages there is space and time enough for me to explore my theme of the secular search for light and innocence.

The use and place of Prometheus and Prometheanism in my discussion is clear enough. But why shall I be talking as much in terms of the metaphor of Orestes and the Oresteia? Let me project this metaphor briefly now and at greater length when the time comes in the body of this book.

At the heart of the secular project there are two movements, intimately and dramatically related. The first is the unending march forward through dead and dank hypotheses to the light of new hypotheses. One of the major marches reviewed by the imagination of Aeschylus in the Oresteia is the march out of the mathematical and mechanical justice of a primitive society into that new world of equity, wisdom, and persuasion which made possible the founding of the city

3

of man. This is only an example, albeit major, of the march forward of the secular project and the march of human resource. All the sciences and all the arts pass through the same process, trying to break out of what is dead and into the new, or out of puzzlement into understanding. Today the explosion into new hypotheses is beyond all measure.

The second movement is always contrary to the first and is caused by it. The brilliant movement forward of Prometheus seems never pure or perfect; amid the beauty and the splendor it cannot at the same time stop generating causes of guilt. Or it cannot endure its own humanity and imperfections. The result is a movement of pause, or a movement backward, or a check, out of guilt and fear. Why, after leading humanity so far forward, is Prometheus in torment upon a lonely Caucasian mountain? Why the enormous torment of conscience and confusion today? We struggle for an answer in either case. The crisis today is partly a wish to correct some of the inhuman qualities of the movement forward; as such it is altogether necessary. But it is also in part a reaction of fear and puritanism in the face of the human project; as such it is purely reactionary.

In the Oresteia there is wave after wave of attempt to move the human situation out of a rigid and dead hypothesis that will no longer work into the light of some new plan, or solution, or possibility. The imagination is trying hard to break out into a new world but cannot do it yet. In that Mycenae of long ago, the house of Atreus was given a tormenting problem which still broods so tragically over the smiling plain of Argos. Some curse, some impossibility, has come upon the house since first Thyestes betrayed his brother, Atreus, and did a deed that must be undone somehow.

How undo this treachery? How solve the problem? How bring the thing to an end satisfactorily, so that there is really a sense of an ending? The answer of Atreus is to strike back at horror with horror; at a great banquet he serves his unknowing brother with the limbs of his own children. These are the ghastly children whom Cassandra is to see in a vision many years later as she reviews all the attempts at an ending that have intervened since then; she now solemnly announces the death of Agamemnon by the instrumentality of two things that come together, the divine curse of Justice and the less than divine axe in the hands of his wife, Clytemnestra. Clytemnestra declares for ending by an axe.

Then comes Orestes to avenge his father and slay his mother, and thus, by the old hypothesis, to bring things again and at last to an end. But it is Orestes, more clearly than any character in the whole trilogy, who comes to cry out the theme of all three plays (and a theme of this book): Where is there an end?

Actually there is a small but growing tendency to rebaptize our age and to call it by the name of the age of Orestes instead of the age of Oedipus. Orestes, for some, has become the symbol of an age that has slain authority and taken on the self-responsibility of the human project. For others—who look to the beautiful ending of reconciliation finally composed by Aeschylus in The Eumenides—he represents the growth and human education of the primitive superego. He is also a new Prometheus.

I can accept the phrase the age of Orestes if allowed to use it in my own sense. I shall be using Orestes as metaphor for the dramatic and painful march of the secular project itself through old hypotheses to new. It can be said that he and every other character in the Oresteia seek two things:

1. They seek at long last a better hypothesis than pure justice to settle human affairs, a better hypothesis for the solving of puzzle or curse. Therefore they seek light.

2. They also seek a pause in that use of any hypothesis which introduces guilt and corruption. Therefore they seek innocence. This is what my own attempt at a dramatic image will have the secular project do.

There is a fascinating similarity between the way the dramatic imagination of an Aeschylus works, through intermediate darkness, rigidities, puzzlements, before breaking into light, and the way in which the philosopher or scientist proceeds. This seems to be especially true of contemporary philosophy. As one commentator describes this bent of modern thought:

> . . . philosophers are not propounding solutions to problems, answering questions, putting forth theories, but are rather grappling with puzzlement, trying to put themselves straight where they are confused; to do philosophy is less like trying to discover some elusive facts than trying to find one's way out of a maze.[1]

As the second play of the trilogy is drawing to a close, Orestes is waving a trap or a net of his own before the audience; he is proclaiming his innocence and the justice of his cause to the world. Has not his mother slain his father with the help of this instrument; is he not right to have slain her, and with the self-same instrument, the self-same trap? Does not perfect justice and violence for violence make a man innocent? But what happens in the next moment? The avenging Furies descend upon him and close upon him the self-same trap, the trap (the hypothesis) the Greek mind was trying to break out of. The Greek mind finally said: It does not work. But we, in our stage of things before we move into our light, are crying out like children: It works! It works! It works!

I wanted to write this book according to the rhythm of a Greek play. Now I see I have begun. As in the prologue of many a Greek play, I have given a good deal of my story and argument away in advance. But if there will be anything worth the saying it will have been worth saying first in a minor way, to strike the theme, and later according to its larger pattern. It is a small risk.

II

The Subject

The religious imagination is in a state of serious division. It is living in a secular world but has no acceptable image of secularity, no image of "the world" within which it can live and breathe.

This book proposes that the religious imagination create an image of the secular project which must do two divergent things. The image must 1) begin with and never abandon the first principles of secularity itself: autonomy, unconditionality, self-identity; 2) yet it must never betray the long-term vocation of the religious imagination, which is to bring total unity to the universe under God and total internal unity to its own imaginings.

In sum, we want an image of secularity which will really be secular and we want an image within which the religious imagination can live and breathe. This is what I set my own hand to. But it should be only one of many such images by many people. The need is very great.

By secularity and the secular project I mean the march of mankind, in the autonomous light of its own resources, toward the mastery and humanization of the world, in the objective terms of all the arts and sciences as these have taken shape and are still taking shape in history. The great symbol of this project was Prometheus, who first gave man fire, then the alphabet, then every other resource by which we have been struggling out of darkness. Up to a certain point in history the project could be seen as an occasional thrust outside a basically religious image of the world. But now it is an overwhelming presence in which the religious imagination must learn to exist. That it must do so and cannot yet do so is almost a definition of the present crisis of the religious imagination. Since the Enlightenment the latter has been in an increasingly divided state. It has been living in two separate worlds.

The modern religious man is also inescapably the secular man, so that the two exacerbating problems—the problem of the religious imagination and the problem of the secular imagination as each faces our new world—have this unity, that they habitually occur within one and the same man. If this were not so, the crisis would be less than it is. The crisis is not the perennial quarrel between the religious man on the one hand and the secular man on the other. Rather, it is the struggle going on in the one man between these apparently diverse principles. Even if he wished it—which he does not—the religious man of our day cannot escape the fact that most of his energies, most of his perspectives, are framed within "the secular project" of the human spirit, within the forward and autonomous movement of human action and history through the arts and sciences, through economics and politics and the whole social reality, toward great but autonomous human goals that have no religious image.

We have been moving through both a major new explosion of energy and frontiers in the modern secular project and a lesser but important explosion of theological literature on the puzzles and crises that have been created thereby for the human spirit. I mention some names in order to bow to them and not to compete with them but to take another road and perform another task. After Bonhoeffer and the creative power that seems to have been hidden in his relatively few aphoristic pages of appeal (in *Letters and Papers from Prison*) for a new religionless Christianity there was: the very great influence of Rudolf Bultmann with his proposals for the demythologizing of Christianity and the centrality of the human self-understanding of Martin Heidegger; Bishop John A. T. Robinson and his criticism of supranaturalism and religiosity in *Honest to God;* the work of Friedrich Gogarten as he relates secularity and the thoughts of Luther himself; the emergence of the death-of-God theology of men like William Hamilton and Thomas J. J. Altizer; the search for a secular meaning of the Gospel by Paul Van Buren; the startling success of Harvey Cox's *The Secular City;* the Catholic work on the critical question of the secular by men like John Metz, Karl Rahner, Richard McBrien. But just as important as the work of a few dozen significant writers and thinkers, there has been the emergence, in the actual world of the secular, of religious activists of every degree who have united vigorous criticism of religious structures with a great zeal for working within the realities of secularity.

My own first few suggestions are that it is both very good and very bad to have declared, so formally and so strikingly, that this movement and crisis is altogether new and altogether important. It is very good because (I shall say it many times) we are almost suddenly in the presence of so vast a secularity that it is a qualitatively new and overwhelming situation for the religious imagination. It is bad because there is often a failure to recognize that we are in a sharply and qualitatively new form of a *permanent human* situation. The debate between man and God over the rights and wrongs of human resource, the search for a human autonomy which need not carry the terrible burden of guilt and alienation, the struggle over the validity or limits or nonlimits of the secular project, is already at fever pitch in the first days of the myth of Prometheus. The more historical a question is, the more deeply human it will turn out to be, even though there are indeed new moments which have a special genius for raising the issue of the freedom of the human project in all its nakedness. There is also a little less danger, if we search for *both* the modern novelty *and* the permanent human and theological reality of the question, that we will have succumbed to a passing movement to which a cynical future will refer as "a theology of secularity from the 1940's to the 1970's." It is therefore better to be alive to the fact that the question of secularity has occurred in other forms before.

One basic proposal of this book is simple. It is that if we begin our question of the relation of the sacred and the secular by telling ourselves and the world what our image (or very human and extended definition) of the secular project is we may thereby settle very many of the issues that seem to be at stake. To build one such image is the whole and only task of the whole book. The hope behind what I try my hand at is the hope behind the logic which says that if you state a problem correctly or imagine a situation correctly, you are on the way to an answer. (Only in this case, I repeat, we need many images by many people.) If we imagine secularity correctly, we will the more easily discover the relation of the sacred to it. I prefer to think that I am talking not with a religious or theological group but with the secular part of my own soul and theirs, or with a secular group that is deeply involved in the secular project. I would not at all expect the latter to say, at the close of the last chapter: "yes, you have given my own image of the project." For the image will be my own and will be an attempt, by healing the divisions in my own modern soul, to objectify and universalize the scars as public scars of the religious imagination. But I would hope that this secular man could come near to saying; "your image is not mine, but it leaves mine intact and has not destroyed me. I can live and breathe and work in it." And I would hope that the secular part of myself would say as much.

If we are to make a new image, then, it would be naïve not to recognize that we are dealing with a very old and permanent problem, whatever the phrases we use to summarize it: faith and the world, Christ and culture, grace and nature, belief and knowledge, God and man, Christianity and civilization. And the problem has a list of towering names that have wrestled with it. However, there should be a few special reasons why so many of us today are so intent on new understandings, new images, of the "nonsacred part of the world."

History of the Problem

First, let me say something very briefly about the history of the problem. I remind myself how vast the tradition of the question is. My own summary is only a brief reminder of the respect I have for it.

So far as central metaphors and images are concerned, I will be dealing with the subject largely in terms of the people and plays that poured out of the dramatic imagination of Aeschylus. His symbolic Prometheus is the father of the secular project; his torment comes from having projected himself into the very center of our question. This initiator of human culture and freedom is told that "Zeus alone is free." He is punished for his assertiveness on behalf of man. Here for the first time the complicated threads of freedom, rebellion, guilt, and the search for innocence in the human project emerge.

Prometheus gives a first explanation of himself to the chorus:

> But you have asked on what particular
> charge Zeus now tortures me. This I will
>   tell you.
> As soon as he ascended to the throne
> that was his father's, straightway he assigned
> to the several Gods their several privileges
> and portioned out the power, but to the unhappy
> breed of mankind he gave no heed, intending
> to blot the race out and create a new.
> Against these plans none stood save I: I dared.
> I rescued men from shattering destruction
> that would have carried them to Hades' house;
> and therefore I am tortured on this rock,
> a bitterness to suffer, and a pain
> to pitiful eyes. I gave to mortal man
> a precedence over myself in pity: I
> can win no pity; pitiless is he
> that thus chastises me, a spectacle
> bringing dishonor on the name of Zeus.[2]

Prometheus is only a first though very great statement of the issue. Greek and Roman civilizations were not "holy" civilizations, but both tended toward a total formalization of life under formally

religious images. We are given a detailed account of this tendency by
Fustel de Coulanges in *The Ancient City*. *The Ancient City* is the
story of that kind of imposition of religious form which prevents or
distorts the emergence of the forms of nature.

In Byzantine culture this tendency may be different but it is
complete. Here Christianity is adopting the same solution for the
question of God and man, sacred and secular. The solution through
the domination of the formally religious image is total. The flood of
history had not yet disturbed this solution. There hardly seems any
difference between the vestments of priest and emperor. Both are
sacred. All is sacred. The two courts are imitations of the heavenly
court. The all-powerful Pantocrator Christ rules the whole world from
that central, consuming point in the ceiling. The terrible Christ of
Daphni, the suburb of Athens, is only a single classical example.

Meanwhile, St. Augustine has composed a book of heroic propor-
tions, *The City of God*, a dramatic image which still powerfully influ-
ences us: two forces, two cities, two histories emerge before us as
ways of reading the world, the earthly city and the city of God,
opposed, wrestling. This is Augustine's way of looking at the world
and reading history. Such images can find no place for an autonomous
secularity, as mine will. But as I look back now at all the stages of
this book I wonder if I have not taken a good portion of my own
images from this remarkable source. I think that St. John in the
Apocalypse, St. Augustine in *The City of God*, and two world wars
have prevented me from drawing a picture of secularity that is naïve
and innocent. The strongest criticism lodged against *The Secular
City* of Harvey Cox is that it has ignored this part of the secular
picture. It has ignored its terror.

At any rate the struggle with the two sides of the question was
there from the beginning. Over against the Alexandrians, the Anti-
ochean part of the Christian tradition was pushing the actual, objective
lines of the created world and the human world further into its religious images and its religious way of looking at the world. And Augustine has told the religious imagination what horrors it is really up
against in its relations with the world.

Is it too much to suggest next that our question is the central
question of philosophy and theology for the whole of the Middle
Ages? It is not necessary to be either glib or presumptuous to ask

this, because it probably strikes quite near to the truth. There are the great explorations into the relations between the omnipotence of God (the universality of the religious presence and meaning) and man's freedom, between grace (as gift of God) and nature (as striving of man), between predestination and human character, between law and nominalism. In its turn the metaphysics of the analogy of being was a remarkable achievement: It created an intelligible, unified universe within which every single difference in nature could emerge in its own right. The painful questions raised by Prometheus are being treated everywhere.

What shall we say of a Dante who had become for Christianity the perfect model of its symbolic genius in interpreting the world within the forms and history of Christianity? It would be a travesty to say that Dante destroyed or distorted a single identity by his poiesis. And he is a poet who can give us overwhelming revelations about ourselves with hardly an effort. "Why is thy mind so entangled," said the master, "that thou slackenest thy pace? What matters it to thee what they whisper here? [We are in Canto v of the *Purgatorio*, where the pilgrim is advancing from one purifying insight to another.] Follow me and let the people talk; stand thou as a firm tower which never shakes its summit for blast of winds: for ever the man in whom thought wells up on thought, sets back his mark, because the one saps the force of the other." Or he has a belief in the pure factuality of evil about which we are so naive. So he describes an evil spirit in terms which could explain several terrible initiators in modern history: "He united that evil will, which seeks ill only, with intellect, and stirred the mist and wind by the power which his nature gave."[3] The realism of Dante is one of the great preludes to what can become our own final realism.[4]

But the area and mode of knowledge called the secular is not the area and the mode of Christian symbolism. Well before beginning my own image of secularity I am indicating some of its central directions. I hope it will not cause horror if I suggest that we must give up Christian symbolism as an instrument for the understanding of our secularity. We cannot take *this* Dantean path.

But if we cannot take *this* path of his, it will be decent of us to remember how much we have learned from him and Aeschylus about the dramatic structure of the mind and the dramatic structure of all insight. As much as anybody else, these two have taught us that our images are not single magical points, but they build themselves realistically, dramatically, in stages. That dramatic mode will be a substantial part of my own method in building a religious image, in stages, of the secular project.

These are only a few of the many milestones in the development of the Promethean question before it broke into the Renaissance as the first of a set of decisive and heroic modern statements of the inner dignity and autonomy of the nonsacred and human world. But my special concern is not so much the history and nature of the secular projects in the succession of epochs like the Renaissance; it is more concern with pairs of moments like the Renaissance and Reformation. Prometheus brings fire to man; Prometheus is then bound. Persia builds a great empire, but then we read in *The Persians* of Aeschylus that it was not so much the Greeks who brought ruin upon this empire at Salamis and Plataea; it was some inner madness in Xerxes and his counselors, and some avenging god. It is as though some innate principle becomes fearful of the movement forward and must trap it into destruction. Yet why should we think that Aeschylus in *The Persians* was talking to anybody but his Athenian audience in the theater of Dionysus? But not all the warnings in the world from the Greek tragedians were able to keep Athens from the same path as the Persians and the same negative counterstory as it is told to us by Thucydides. The beautiful energies of the Athenians move into a position of guilt, cruelty, exploitation of the surrounding world, and into a blindness that matches the blindness of Xerxes, Oedipus, Ajax, Heracles, Creon, Pentheus, Jason, and all the other tragic figures who had walked the stage so clearly before them, going to doom by the path of their single-minded strength. One of the steady images the religious imagination has formed of the secular project is a fearful image compounded of such historical pairs of events and historical rhythms. (Bonhoeffer saw quite clearly that this was one habitual way the religious imagination had of imagining "the world").

The Renaissance explodes into a miracle of human energy and achievement; the Reformation, in great part a radical and guilty criticism of the new leap forward, follows close on its heels. I cannot possibly say anything adequate about the labor spent on our question from that time to our own: through Nicholas of Cusa, Campanella,

Luther, Bellarmine, the men of the Enlightenment, Hegel (for some say he is the quintessential image of modern man's self-asssertion), Kierkegaard, Schleiermacher, Ritschl, Tolstoy, Barth, to the Bonhoeffer of a few years ago. Among all these and many more it is hardly possible to find a strong assertion on behalf of man without finding as strong a counterassertion. But again it may be helpful to think of this cycle of action and reaction as a drama taking place in the interior soul of all of us at a given epochal moment. Thus understood we would not be examining situations where half a world goes forward with giant strides in the sciences and the arts while the other half refuses. There is some truth to that, but it is also true that both action and reaction belong in some permanent way to the heart of the secular project itself. Let us hypothesize that you cannot have one without the other.

This may contribute to explaining what is happening at our present moment of European and American history. We are again at the height of an extraordinary era of human achievement. But the reaction has already set in, this time with violent energy and rage. In part the reaction fears the step forward; in part it knows that the step forward must be purified of its negative and nonhuman elements; in the bargain the reaction cannot control its guilt; I think it is bewildered by its own feelings; it proposes that the whole project be torn down. Thus I am proposing the possibility that our revolution of the moment is not a progressive situation; rather it is a moment of reaction and bewilderment within the secular project. It is a search for innocence. And one searches for what one does not have.

New Dimensions of the Problem Today

We can say, without any criticism of the past, that the religious imagination needs a new image of the secular project because it is in the presence of what is altogether a new form of the problem of "the world." On the surface the new factor is purely quantitative and therefore not new at all; the new factor is the extraordinary and overwhelming dimensions of secularity as it has developed in the last two hundred years. Still more extraordinary is the range it has developed in the past fifty years. Secularity always has meant independent and autonomous factuality: Things are what they are or can be. This world has declared, since the days of the Enlightenment, that it is not helped by religious meaning. Nevertheless the religious consciousness had always insisted that finally there was no real meaning without religious meaning; it had continued to impose its own meanings on the beginnings of this world. It had done this by symbol and by transcendental references of the secular facts to something outside of themselves.

But the new dimensions of secularity really create a qualitatively new situation. The past did indeed have our problem but it did not have the suffering and bewilderment that go with this qualitatively new version of secularity. We used to ask the question: What is the place of the secular in a totally religious world? Now, overwhelmed, we more often phrase the question thus: What is the place of the sacred in an overwhelmingly secular world? If the religious imagination stays within its older images of symbolic, referential, and transcendent meaning it will be forced to accept the image of defeat. I do not mean the defeat of Christ, which it has always preached. I mean the pure and flat defeat called real inconsequence. It will be confirmed in something that begins to be its self-image: It is the image of an ever widening secularity of autonomous meaning pushing the religious imagination into a narrower and narrower corner of civilization. Thus, as secularity (S) extends its walls, the religious image (R) feels its walls closing in more and more narrowly upon itself.

And this will remain the truth for us in the absence of a new image of secularity.

It is no longer viable to say that we can and must change the relative dimensions of this situation. Rather we must explore the hypothesis that the religious imagination, while remaining a religious imagination, can create a new image of secularity whose first stage will be the acceptance of secularity. This is what we should mean by the new theological phrase "taking the secular risk." The supposition would not be the defeat and the death, the passivity, of the religious imagination; the supposition would rather be that the latter would take the active role of forcing secularity to become really itself. It must not be a balancing tension; it must be a creative force.

If the new dimensions of secularity constitute a real crisis for the religious consciousness and are our first reason for a new image, the second reason, when juxtaposed to the first, is ironic and quite different. If secularity is now in an unrivaled position as our dominant form of knowledge and behavior, it is also true that it too is in a state of crisis. The fact is that if the religious imagination is in a bad way, the secular imagination is just as badly off. Who can deny that there is a vast unhappiness in the secular air about the state of the secular project?

It is difficult to say exactly what is happening. On the surface it is a vast reaction against structures and against every manner of establishment. The crisis of the secular imagination is quite different from that of the religious imagination. The religious imagination must still struggle with the very idea of secularity. But that is not the case with its secular counterpart. For the secular imaginer, the man of vision in the secular order, has no trouble with the idea of secularity. Quite the contrary. From the days of the Renaissance, the Enlightenment, the high days of romanticism, he has been increasingly possessed by a fascinating vision of secularity. It is not the idea itself, it is the corruption of this secular idea, the failure of this idea to achieve itself, that is the principal cause of his pain. For example, he wants man and his world to become more and more human, but he finds himself surrounded by dehumanizing processes. Confronted with what he deems to be a tawdry and nonhuman reality, the secular imaginer is haunted by his ideal image. Herbert Marcuse in his *One-Dimensional Man* takes melodramatic advantage of this situation. He knows very well that this is the dialectical process going on, this struggle between the *is* and the *ought*, the fact and the ideal. He puts his finger on the dialectical struggle between the two images and the torment that results. The trouble is that he is not dialectical enough. His dialectic is too external. It projects the whole problem upon the System. He divides the world into good guys and bad guys, and thus he establishes guilt in one group and innocence in another.

Though he uses solemn Hegelian terms he makes a simple Western out of the whole complicated picture. The search for innocence is, fortunately, more complicated than this.

I, too, will propose that there is a dramatic and dialectical process going on at the very heart of this secular project, this project of human resource, this project of the arts and sciences. But it is not as simple a process as Marcuse suggests. No doubt there are especially corrupted groups, but that is a secondary problem. The search for innocence lies finally at the heart of the secular project itself. It is the project itself which, since Prometheus, is filled with intolerable fantasies, with the most terrible aggressions and terrors, with the perpetual wish to settle for some cheap imitation of its own ideal. It is the project itself that is in search of innocence.

POLARITY OF THE SECULAR IMAGE

There are many images of the secular project abroad, but it may be helpful to conceive of them as stretching across a spectrum between two severely polarized images of the project. I shall try to summarize this polarized situation.

At the one pole there is a love and admiration of energy, power, greatness, genius, and all the forms these splendid things can produce. At the opposite pole there is a deep distrust of this energy and genius —a fear, almost a hatred, of the great world they are always building. But it is possible that there is an alliance, a secret cousinship, between this polarity of sheer energy and sheer destruction. Perhaps it is a unilinear sense of power behind both the building and the destroying, behind the feeling of creation and the feeling of guilt, that unites the pair. It is very difficult, therefore, to separate the two, the energy and the guilt. But this is what must be done.

At any rate, we tend at one pole of our image of secularity to become obsessed with energy and power, as though we do not know how to modify or give some human density to this image. At the other pole we become preoccupied with a puritanical guilt about powers and with the wish to destroy it. Let me first say something further about the preoccupation with energy and power. Two things are clear about energy and power: that they are magnificent things and that they must be mastered by and within human forms. We do not quite realize how much they are on our minds, how much they are part of our character, how much they penetrate many areas where they do not belong at all. The better examples of this should be come by indirectly. We have enough direct testimony, enough of a bibliography, on our image of power and life, but it is more interesting to catch it where we never thought to. That fine American critic of Renaissance art, Bernard Berenson, for example, is almost trapped into nonsense and a Nietzschean caricature as he limits the task of Michelangelo and the whole of art to the enhancement of life and energy. It is a sudden shock to read that it was absurd of Michelangelo to paint a man on a crucifix with head down and feet up.

Now humility and patience were feelings as unknown to Michelangelo as to Dante before him, or—for that matter, to any other of the world's creative geniuses at any time. Even had he felt them, he had no means of expressing them, for his nudes could convey a sense of power, not of weakness; of terror, not of dread; of despair but not of submission. . . . Michelangelo therefore failed in his conception of the subject [of the Last Judgment], and could not but fail. But where else in the world of art shall we receive such blasts of energy as from this giant's dream, or, if you will, nightmare. For kindred reasons, the "Crucifixion of Peter" is a failure. Art can only be life-communicating and life-enhancing. If it treats of pain or death, these must always appear as manifestations and as results only of living resolutely and energetically. What chance is there, I ask, for this, artistically the only possible treatment, in the representation of a man crucified with his head downwards.[5]

We read again and again of the incredible energy of the mighty figures of Greek tragedy, Oedipus, Ajax, Philoctetes, Antigone, Heracles, Electra. But by some miracle this energy and autonomous power is seen to be present and undaunted as much after defeat as before. One of the prevailing images western man has of himself is of a creature who must live and die unbowed and unsubmissive to the world; it is one of the great stances of Prometheus. This is fine, but it is a polarity, it is not the whole of life. Also, I believe it to be an intellectual image, an image the intellectual forms of life. By some paradox the poor man, poorer in body and spirit, is often able to live within wider and truer images and does not suppose that even a tired death must be swallowed up by a romantic energy that now actually is not there. It is in this spirit that I cite with wonderment this recurring understanding of the magic heroes of old, this time from Bernard Knox, one of our best Sophoclean critics.

> The Sophoclean hero acts in a terrifying vacuum, a present which has no future to comfort and no past to guide, an isolation in time and space which imposes on the hero the full responsibility for his own action and its consequences. It is precisely this fact which makes possible the greatness of the Sophoclean heroes; the source of their action lies in them alone, nowhere else; the greatness of the action is their's alone. Sophocles presents for the first time what we recognize as a "tragic hero"—one who, unsupported by the Gods and in the face of human opposition, makes a decision which springs from the deepest layer of his individual nature, his *physis*, and then blindly, ferociously, heroically maintains that decision even to the point of self-destruction.[6]

Knox himself heroically holds to the image in both of his books on the subject. Another Sophoclean scholar, Cedric H. Whitman, produces a counterpart image of this great individual who will defeat the malignity of the world and fortune. "And this involves a contrast between the man who yields to what he feels to be necessity [Odysseus] and the man [Ajax] who yields to nothing because his own Arete is for him the only divinity which can control him morally."[8]

I wish, at this stage, to make my point briefly or I would go on with the recording of this permanent Promethean streak in our self-image. There is the enormous responsibility for the whole world that Jean-Paul Sartre and Simone de Beauvoir place upon the moral shoulders of all of us. One needs vast shoulders and muscles for such responsibility. We are all condemned to be Titans, bearing the responsibility for the whole world. We are told that everything that happens is our own responsibility or fault. This may be humility of a kind, but it is surely not a very modest humility. There is a kind of monumentality to it that would require the genius of Michelangelo himself to sketch.

But, if there are such monumental images of secular man, there is at the other pole a deep fear and hatred of them. There are forces in us that hold these images in contempt and that attack them with irony, parody, mockery. Most of these forces are indispensable to man. But the strongest of them all is a destructive puritanism that seems to have as much strength as the very thing it attacks. It is now a distinct and very visible force among us. It is a kind of Prometheanism in reverse. There is bound to be trouble when titanism and guilt come in the same package.

However, it is not only the stature or the monumentality of the project that may be agitating these minds and consciences, and at the right time we shall have to look into other factors. There is the frequent inhumanity of the project—its nonhuman qualities. There is its eternal link with aggression. There is also, probably, a real fear of the principle of autonomy in secularity.

At any rate this is no time for the religious imagination to come through with an overly glib or simplistic image of the secular project. If it does so, a frightened and confused secular imagination may laugh it out of court.

I am suggesting that one of the major complications in the picture is this rather extraordinary combination of the building and the destroying strains in contemporary Prometheanism. It is not melodramatic—because the picture is so clear—to say that it is a period of enormous energy and of enormous contempt. For the human mind it is the greatest of all the building and exploring periods. It is also a period of remarkable autonomy for the secular project. But the other half of the picture is this equally extraordinary and, we often fear, so equally powerful drive toward absolute contempt and parody. No single metaphor for the representation of this reality will satisfy everyone. If we choose a dramatic metaphor we call it the age of Pirandello. I for one think we must distinguish between Pirandello and Pirandellism, because it seems to me that the Italian playwright was often the most compassionate of students of the use of masks, defenses, and relative viewpoints by muddling human beings; the classical picture drawn of him by Adriano Tilgher seems an exaggeration and itself a mask.[9] But the thing now called Pirandellism became a consuming reality which attacked the substance of everything and discovered nothing but mask under mask under mask; it made a profession of mixing reality and illusion; not only mockery of reality but self-mockery was an essential part of this new artist.

The effect of Pirandellism on a long line of artists in the theater cannot be questioned; witness the examples of Genêt, Giraudoux, Sartre, Brecht, Anouilh, Ionesco, Pinter, Miller. At the end of Arthur Miller's last play *The Price* there is nothing much left of the mask of the good son. At the end of *Death of a Salesman* there is nothing much left of the American masks of Willy Loman. The ironic thing is that if we go back to a reading of *To Clothe the Naked*, a fairly representative play by Pirandello himself, we find that if there are villains on the stage the villains are those who do the unmasking of Ersilia. Ersilia finally tells them:

> So here I am at last. Are you all satisfied? And now leave me alone. . . . Go away and let me die in silence—naked. Please go. I have a right to say it now, don't I? That I don't want to see anyone. Or talk to anyone. Go, go and tell your wife—tell your fiancée —that this corpse—yes—this corpse died naked.[10]

There is a great gap between this and Pirandellism. But even the latter—however heroic an unmasker of people and of apparent substance it became—has become a rank amateur in the face of the new revolutionaries. The new mastery of mockery is, by ambition, without limit.

This energy and this mockery are now in a state of confrontation within the secular project. The confrontation is being played out in many ways. It is being played out in the openness of many historical forms, partly, for example, in the form of cultural and class conflicts and styles of life. But though it is not right to reduce history to psychology or to spirituality, it is also true that this confrontation is being acted out in the interior of the individual, as a psychological and a spiritual problem. The man who chooses to handle this moment of history by contempt is also dealing, when he does this, with the most powerful and positive human energies and wishes of his own soul. He too has a divided imagination. The secular imagination is as divided as the religious.

III

Definitions

Let me give a set of definitions of key words and phrases in the vocabulary I am already using or will be using. But I will not ask the reader to live through even a short section of pure definitions. I will choose only those which will initiate or advance the discussion. And the form I give the definitions will be very free and flexible.

A first objective of these definitions will be to bring clarity to the nature of our older and classical religious images of the world and secularity. The hypothesis is that we need "a new religious image." But this does not make too much sense unless we define "the old religious image." Again, I shall be saying that our new image must take as its first phrase the constitutive "unconditionality" of secularity. The word *unconditionality* will not emerge with too much clarity if we have not previously analyzed the *conditional* quality of our older images. When the new image makes its formal beginning it will be asking that the old image move abruptly across an abyss from a religiously conditioned image to what seems a nonreligious world with no conditions save its own. That abyss will seem like many things: It will seem nonreligious, a descent into hell on the part of the religious consciousness. But that will be clear only if we understand the past and all that is now being asked of the past.

There are also more fundamental words which must not be taken for granted. Two such words could not be simpler. They are *imagination* and *image*. These words will not be used in eccentric ways, but neither is my use of them quite ordinary. Since the word *imagination* has so many meanings, what do I mean when I use the word? And what is so important about an *image* that the presence or the absence of an image can be a critical matter for the religious consciousness?

IMAGINATION

It is indeed hard to see why an image of the secular world can be so important as to reach a point of crisis; it is hard to see this unless something extraordinary is contained in the reality behind the word *image* and the word *imagination*.

The use of these two words does not mean that we are dealing with an aesthetic problem, or that we want to deal *aesthetically* with a pair of serious situations. As I use the word, the imagination is not an aesthetic faculty. It is not a single or special faculty. It is all the resources of man, all his faculties, his whole history, his whole life, and his whole heritage, all brought to bear upon the concrete world inside and outside of himself, to form images of the world, and thus to find it, cope with it, shape it, even make it. The task of the imagination is to imagine the real. However, that might also very well mean making the real, making the world, for every image formed by everybody is an active, creative step, for good or for bad. The religious imagination now lives in an intermediate state. It is unhappy with its image of the secular, which is an image of its own making, and the unhappiness is a step forward. But it does not yet know what it wants. The religious imagination is at a standstill. It is in a net or trap. But deep down it is bubbling over with tremendous energy as it looks for the beginnings of a new image. Everything, the very shape of our future world, depends upon what the image will be. If the right people do not imagine the world, somebody else always will. Accordingly, very many people are setting themselves to this task.

The religious imagination shapes man and the world according to their final and total meanings. The religious imagination, given certain resources, tries literally to imagine things with God. Again and again, therefore, it finds itself rearranging patterns of facts and evidence into new patterns, according to its own information, its own forms, its own history. It pours everything that it knows and wants into its own patterns. It says simply: This is the way I see things.

The imagination is really the only way we have of handling the world. It is at the point of the imagination, at the precise point where an image is formed, that we meet the world, deal with it, judge it.

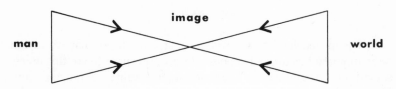

man — image — world

If this is so, then we can say that the imagination wrestles with the world, and that it truly suffers. The religious imagination suffers in transitional periods when it is under the necessity of forming a new and central image. This imagination is going through its Promethean story all over again. It also knows now that this secular Titan, this rank outsider and pretender, is not really such but is somehow a part of itself, trying to be born. One thinks of other metaphors, of the prisoners of Michelangelo, struggling to break out of marble, out of bonds, out of darkness. But thus far it is also difficult for the religious imagination to see the giant that is newly there as anything but a cancerous growth. The present inadequate images of "the world" are part of the suffering of the religious imagination. It is justly fearful of losing its own soul in the process of imagining.

Once again Aeschylus can be our guide here. For his description of a triple stage in every tragic action makes much sense. He tells us in the Agamemnon that every such story begins with a plunge into action (e.g. Prometheus steals fire and gives it to man); the action meets reality, has every manner of unforeseen consequence, and passes through a suffering history; through suffering the action reaches a new insight, or point of reconciliation. These words summarize all: drama, pathos, mathos.

Thus, according to the same rhythm, the religious imagination moves into the secular world, as it knows it must (it acts). One of the principal forms of the suffering that follows is that which comes from the series of images in terms of which it tries to give sense to its entrance; finally, hopefully, there is relief in a new image or hypothesis. I shall elaborate on this triple process at some length in a later chapter. Meantime, I merely remind that Kenneth Burke and Francis Fergusson have done considerable work in developing this Aeschylean structure of the dramatic imagination for us.[11] Let me give a free-running definition of the word image.

IMAGE

If the imagination is the whole of us struggling, through images, with the world, then our images are not the innocent, purely objective things they seem to be. The most casual image contains the whole of man. Images are not snapshots of reality. They are what we have made of reality. Everything in us pours into the simplest image. They are ourselves.

I do not believe in the possibility of a pure sensation, a pure experience, or a pure image that can be isolated from the rest of the life of man. There is a growing literature dealing with the co-presence to our images of endless factors in the human spirit.[12] This development became a central part of modern historical thought, in Bradley, Dilthey, Collingwood, and others who began to reject the possibility of a purely objective fact in history which is not seen, selected, interpreted, and reinterpreted by men.

All of our principal and habitual images have an extraordinary range and content that only emerges into awareness under analysis or in a period of emergency. This is true of the image we have of a man, a woman, a child, birth, life, death, morning, night, food, friend, the enemy, the self, the human, the world as world, the secular world that immediately surrounds us. These images are packed with experience, history, concepts, judgments, decisions, wishes, hopes, disappointments, love, and hate. And all this gets into the actual concrete visible, audible, tactile stuff of our images. Thus one cannot get closer to a man, nor can a man get closer to himself, than through his images. They not only come at us from the world; we also come at the world through them, in love or hate. We can make or destroy the world with an image.

STRIPPING OF IMAGES

Either one of several problems may develop according to the ways in which the imagination deals with the content of its images. The content may be too much and may need emptying, stripping (today we are going through vast and painful periods of the stripping of images); or the content may be too little and may need more imagining.

An image can be overweighted with a content that it should not have. We may be packing images with materials that do not belong to them. This is, in fact, one of the basic suppositions of psychoanalytic theory and practice—namely, that the images of the present can be symbolically packed with the past and that there is no other cure for such a situation than a process of desymbolization. The religious imagination is faced with an analogue of this situation, faced, that is to say, with the need of a vast desymbolizing process, as it tries to construct its secular image. And this, too, will at first have all the feelings of a "descent into hell" as this imagination puts off old habits and takes the "risk of secularity." (Its symbols will return but not before taking this risk).

As an example of what I mean, it will have to stop seeing the form of Christ in everything; it will have to reject the Byzantine Christ, the Pantocrator; the ruler and dominator of all things; the great Christ who consumes the whole building, and thus the whole world, with his own form: It will have to choose not a consuming but a creative Christ, who lets secularity come into its own form and life. Thus, if I were asked how the religious imagination must imagine the world, I would answer that its *first* step may be a stripping process that almost resembles not imagining. This is a terrible discipline for the imagination. It is part of its descent into hell.

There are many clear senses today in which both the religious and the secular imagination are passing and must pass through these vast desymbolizing and stripping processes. Certainly these processes have always been a major part of the vocation of the human imagination. Nobody could do more than suggest the range of the literary texts that have shared this task in history. Tragic literature has always done it in a special way; it has perennially led the imagination out of everyday images of everyday grandeur and easy forms of energy into the reality of human finitude and weakness. And here, no one has been more severe or straight than Sophocles. I skip the more obvious examples for the seldom discussed case of the tragic Creon in the *Antigone*, the Creon who cries out to the gods that he was already dead from grief when they chose to smite him again in a terrible way and to reveal the blind creature under the great king. . . . All this is true of literary history, and an endless series of other strippings, but still there is something unique about our own time as it has raised this vocation to a central and defining quality of its own imagination. In part, but only in part, this work has been nihilistic, an absolute attack on every kind of form and system. But, only in part. In greater part it has been an attack on forms that have come to hide or conceal existence. On the surface it is not creative, but this judgment can itself hide a singularly limited understanding of creativity.

THE OLD IMAGE: CONDITIONALITY

The religious imagination will have to empty itself of some of its images as it imagines secularity. In other cases there will not be so much an emptying as a shifting of images. For example, there will more likely be a shift in its classical emphasis on the conditionality of the world. Let us pause to honor the great tradition and to summarize it in a necessarily inadequate way.

The older religious images are of two kinds:

1. There is a long tradition of superb and positive images of "the world" which range from great symbolic achievement to extremely sophisticated and difficult metaphysical solutions, none of which faced the absolute fact of secularity because it was not yet there in range sufficient to create our problem.

2. There is another and negative set of religious images of secularity; they are more passive reactions to the movement of history and cultural situations than new attempts to match the positive work of the past. They represent the secular in terms of the defeat of the sacred, the disappearance of the gods, the conquest of the desert over green lands, the land of the absurd, the death of God.

I will summarize a whole series of the great images of the past under the word *conditionality*.

On the whole, the older religious image of the world could not tolerate the basic secular notion of *constitutive* autonomy and unconditional, self-contained novelty. It had to relate everything to a center, to a principle or condition outside itself. Indeed, this relationship could be said to be the meaning of a thing. A purely secular fact was considered not to have meaning. Religion cannot remain religion nor God God, if it does not include *everything* in its meaning and if it is not able to give its meaning to everything. Nor can religion accept an equality of meaning from any other system. Our problem is: How can we accomplish the same objective and still remain secular?

Such a conditioned image or meaning required a line of relationship between all things and God. Everything is conditional and relational. Under this general form of meaning and image we can list many sub-phases and propositions:

All things find their meaning in terms of the glory of God.

All things are a means to a final end.

All creatures are a ladder to God.

All things should at least be capable of some symbolic meaning by which they symbolize another and a higher principle.

All nature must in some way or other be supernaturalized.

Historical Christianity must impose its own historical forms, events, meanings upon nature and natural history.

The fact and event of Christ is a new and historical form which shall be imposed, for meaning's sake, upon all things.

Likewise, all things shall finally be found to reflect him.

If a thing does not have transcendental meaning, it has no meaning and is absurd.

The world is hierarchical and climbs from meaning to meaning.

There is, therefore, a deep conditionality at the heart of all things.

This sense and image of things has helped to create many great civilizations and cultures.

Let us repeat that the conditional religious image and idea was frequently able to grasp and develop the deepest, roughest forms of particularity and individuality, in both symbol and speculation. I have given the merest sketch of some of this noble history in the first part of this prologue. But conditionality and relationship had to get constitutively into the image or the idea, somehow. There was the frequent supposition that the interior meaning of a thing must be received, confirmed, reinforced by means of participation in a form like but more perfect than itself. The religious imagination had not yet been asked to meet the problem of absolute inner unconditionality in the constitutive meaning of a thing. The question arose as a great question with the Enlightenment. The Enlightenment has declared ever since that it did not need the religious hypothesis.

But let there be no mistake about it. This is not an exclusive problem of the religious imagination, this drive toward and need of conditionality. I repeat that unconditionality has also become part of the task of the secular imagination. But it is a confusing task. When Jean-Paul Sartre asks us in *Nausea*, in the name of authenticity, to put aside layer after layer of meanings that have been imposed on things, and to remove every social layer of interpretation, so that we be faced with the sheer unexplainable existence of chairs, people, and the roots of trees, he suggests nausea as the only possible reaction. And others say despair and suicide. In *The Brothers Karamazov* of Dostoevski, Ivan Karamazov is sure that if there is no God, then everything is permitted. Again there would be no difference or meaning in things-in-themselves. These are only passing instances. What needs further exploration is our broad psychology of parody and mockery, as though there is nothing that can stand up under its own unconditioned weight. There seems to be some kind of inner battle going on at the heart of secularity between a magnificent ideal of high unconditionality on the one hand and a spirituality of universal parody on the other. The latter part of the battle has been caught superbly by Thomas Mann through the character of Adrian Leverkühn in his *Doctor Faustus*. This spirituality of mockery is often demonic, and the present revolutionary is a good deal caught in it. This is what many forms of unconditionality often mean, as much to the secular as to the religious imagination.

DEMYTHOLOGIZING

On the other hand an image or a set of images may have been flattened out by the absence of what should be there. The content is a "too little" and not a "too much" (though both can be true at the same time). This is more likely to be a great part of the problem of the secular imagination as it strives for an image of itself. It has been a notable achievement of the human spirit to have been able to separate the secular from the sacred, to dedivinize the secular world, to drive the gods and the absolutes out of it. The descriptions of this dedivinizing process in the opening chapters of Harvey Cox's The Secular City are the fascinating parts of that book. Among other things this process has made possible the whole development of modern science; it has given new forms of freedom to the imagination in the arts; it has helped us solve the church-state problem. But the process has gone too far and thus created a new set of problems. The new problems can center around a definition of the word demythologizing as I shall use it.

For the process in question has also taken the magnificence out of the secular order; it has taken the tragedy and the sense of nothingness out of it; it has taken the horror out of it; it has not only dedivinized it, it has often reduced it to a machine and made possible the emergence of these tawdry caricatures and parodies of itself which we now protest against. We can with gratitude accept the dedivinization of secularity, but the real problem is how to restore the image of its grandeur and its terror. I think that this act of restoration will have very important consequences for theology. For a good deal of what has happened in contemporary theology vis-a-vis the secular might be described in the following way:

Not only was the secular order dedivinized; a vast wave of reductionism set in, in terms of which the secular was reduced to the one-dimensional and the purely mechanical and the nonhuman. Of course this creates a crisis, and religion is called upon to make itself relevant to the agony that must follow. But relevant to what? Not relevant to a magnificent reality but to a "demythologized," a de-visioned order of things. In the name of relevance, therefore, theology is asked to demythologize itself, to drop its own "irrelevant" resources, to forget its own historical imagination. Thus the first act of demythologizing did not take place in theology or religion. It took place in the secular order, in such a way that the true dignity of the secular idea is now in danger of collapsing. It is in terms of making itself relevant to this ghost that religion is invited to "demythologize" itself. But what would this mean save that an abstraction should make itself relevant to an abstraction. Despite every corruption of its true image, the *real* secular project remains a magnificent ideal, and the confrontation with it by a demythologized theology, a theology that had surrendered all its own inner resources, would become the confrontation of a pygmy with a giant.

This is the trap that has to be avoided on both sides, by both the religious and the secular imagination. The trap would be that Christ and Prometheus meet each other on the lowest possible level of confrontation, after each had surrendered his highest and best self. This would be a long way from the quality of the confrontation between Zeus and Prometheus in the imagination of Aeschylus.

I would like to point out the paradox I have initiated by proposing: 1) that the religious imagination should give up its own forms as ways of interpreting the secular; 2) that the religious imagination must not become a pygmy by surrendering its own resources. I shall have to deal carefully with this paradox at the proper time.

Negative Religious Image of the Secular

Nor has the religious imagination itself been without fault in devalorizing the image of secularity. We have seen that it has had an altogether understandable wish and need to relate everything to itself and to impose its own forms upon the world as final meaning. But I have less sympathy and less understanding for another drive in the religious imagination. Fortunately this drive—toward the devalorization of the secular order—is more occasional, more adventitious, and not native to the older religious image. Nevertheless it has exercised a very powerful influence on our total image of secularity.

Again and again the religious artist has chosen to confirm the negative image of the secular, almost to the point of being happy about the whole situation. Since there was anxiety about the priority of the supernatural and religious order, there was an allocation of everything good and *really* human to the sacred, of everything mean and without true depth or humanity to the secular. In France we have a long series of Christian writers, including Bloy, Bernanos, Mauriac, Julien Green, who were passionately dedicated to this kind of vision. In England we have the examples of Evelyn Waugh and Graham

Greene. Who more than the last named is as devoted to the image of the secular as completely empty? He has given us a new set of metaphors to fill out this basic principle that a ton of the secular is not worth an ounce of the sacred. But let us have a taste of the detail of his basic metaphor of the secular order. One of my own later metaphors of secularity may make it a place of horror, but the Greene metaphor never lets it rise to that point of dignity.

Again and again the Greene locale is a humid colonial country where the world, and the souls of men with it, just rots and rots and rots. Time after time it is a place of sordid heat where only the mad would really wish to move. On the first page of A Burnt-Out Case we read that: "There was not enough air to stir the fringes of his beard," and "If no change means peace, this certainly was peace. . . ." There follow a cupboard where the cockroaches lurk, and houses built on stilts to guard against rain and rats. One can hear vampire bats creaking over the forest. "I've come to an end," says the burnt-out case. "This place, you might say, is the end. Neither the road nor the river go any further." The man feels he cannot love and never has. He hates his success ("Success is like that too—a mutilation of the natural man").[13] He died, laughing at nobody but himself. But there is the constant question of Graham Greene: Perhaps the rest of the world is corrupt. But it is in a corruption that is at least bothered by belief that Greene finds the saints.

I shall stay for but a few lines with The Heart of the Matter, where the world of Scobie also rots and rots in the same climatic metaphors. His soul rots with pity, with pity for his wife and pity for another woman; it is almost the mark of the climate itself that he cannot choose. Finally he stands outside the whole actual world of choice and offers his damnation to God. Does all this also hide a secret saint? The world may rot, and we with it, but there is a secret point of sparkle. Outside of the sparkling point is the secular world.

With Greene there is a stylistic quality which separates salvation from the world or brings it in adventitiously. He is absorbed with the problem of belief, but it is an absorption that often comes in the back gate of life and style; the entertainment does not quite support it. We are not altogether sure that Brown, in The Comedians, should suddenly say: "The first colors touched the garden, deep green and then deep red—transience was my pigmentation; my roots would never go deep enough to make me a home or make me secure with love."[14] The world gets divided between the tragedians who believe in something and the comedians who don't. And what generally passes for the secular world never comes off very well. This is all very fine, and it is hard to question it until one remembers the implication that it does not very much matter what goes on in the secular world since it does not have certain forms of commitment. Neither does it much matter what kind of a world the sacred is as long as it is sacred.

I shall let the Greene case go at that, but I think the same situation can be verified for a good number of writers in this tradition. Perhaps it holds for the whole tradition among us, after Eliot, of the world as wasteland, a tradition which often went beyond historical cultural criticism and became a metaphysical summary of the world.

DIALECTICAL THEOLOGY

There are many other factors that have contributed to the degraded image of secularity. There is a long tradition of the religious writer who allocated all that was good to the sacred and nothing but the flat, the neutral and the nonhuman to the secular. On the Protestant side the same dark colors or lack of color emerged for the secular as one of the main consequences of the *dialectical theology*. What is dialectical theology? Any book on the subject will contain an equivalent of the following two sentences: "But what is the nature of dialectical theology? The answer to that question is not altogether simple." At any rate it always takes the form of sharp contrariety and paradox. "Dialectical theology is the mode of thinking which defends this paradoxical character, belonging to faith-knowledge, from the non-paradoxical speculations of reason, and vindicates it as against the other."[15]

Thus the function of theology is to set forth truths that stand in contradiction one to the other: the allness of God and the nothingness of man, the Gospel and the Law, God and the world, the presence of God reached only in the absence of God, salvation only in despair, creation through destruction. Thus conceived, dialectic becomes especially modern, because the modern loves to unite opposites.

What must concern us here is the degree to which dialectical theology may have been founded in our day, not on a theological principle or method, but on the basis of modern cultural history and the actual degenerative state of the secular idea and the finite human world. The proposal has been made that the history of modern dialectical theology, from Søren Kierkegaard to Karl Barth, is not so much a theology as it is a religious image of modern culture.[16] But even if this is true, it has helped to sanctify and give theological status to the degenerative image of secularity.

It is time we stopped enjoying our negative images of secularity. The price of the fun is much greater than "the risk of secularity" in a new image of the secular.

IMAGE AND METHOD

Now we come to the task of composing a new image of secularity. My own image will be composed of a series of elements, moments, or phases, and thus will not be a complete image until the series of elements is completed. I will begin in Act One with the element of secular autonomy and unconditionality as a central piece in the image, but with the understanding that our imagining only begins there. The image we are building is progressive in the most literal sense; it proceeds through many stages and requires the whole book for its creation. (And the book will only be a shorthand sketch of the real content of an image of secularity.) But I do not locate some single central point as the heart of my image and then force all other elements under it—as sub-images under one great image or as species under a genus. I use a Platonic understanding of a unity and this is freer and more flexible.[17] It allows each phase of a definition or an image to be itself a unity, a point, a perspective, that makes sense in its own right and that can stand on its own two feet. No subsequent element will cancel out a prior element in the image. Thus there will be any number of steps that will follow upon the opening phase of secular unconditionality and autonomy, but never in such a way as to cancel out the whole unconditional method of modern thought. No doubt each stage modifies every other, but each keeps its own importance. And since new facts keep pouring in upon us, there will never be a final phase of this image; it must be kept open.

In the spirit of this methodology, I begin, I repeat, by allowing those powerful qualities of autonomy, independence, and unconditionality to emerge within the secular image. (And the complete acceptance of these qualities will involve a kind of descent into hell for the religious imagination as the latter strips itself of its own meanings, history, and symbols in order to allow full secularity to be born.) But nothing will be taken from these free and interior principles of the project if we see that this step involves the redemptive emergence, on their own terms, of all the things and people which are brought to light within the project. For the religious imagination this first step is the beginning of a dramatic action which now involves other acts and stages.

In our next stage we must proceed to imagine a secular project that is not only human but is also totally human. The true unconditionality and freedom of secularity will not suffer if we imagine that it must now pass through human laws and ways. The weakness of Promethean energy is that it is only *part* of the human. We will see that the characters of Samuel Beckett belong as much to the secular project as does Prometheus himself, the bringer of fire. In this stage of our dramatic action I also sketch an image of the unconditionality of the human imagination over against the unconditionality of the will or pure "Prometheanism." And at this "moment" of the image the once purely *mechanical* secular becomes a world of good and evil, of principalities and powers. The dramatic movement is growing. We have now moved from secular project to human project, from cosmocentric to anthropocentric view, from mechanism to world of good and evil.

If now the length and movement of my image begins to be clear, I can afford to be briefer from this point—for a summary is only a summary. In the next section (Act Two) I imagine the secular project as a constant search for light through the dramatic Aeschylean movement of action, suffering, and insight (or through the movement of old hypothesis, passage through a suffering stage of puzzlement or pain, and the reaching to the light of a new hypothesis). It is also a march through freedom. In a fundamental sense the project will be eternal, and the search for light will be infinite.

Then, in a final act, I imagine our project as a constant search for innocence. So important is this section of the image for me, and so important is *this* search today, that I nearly named the book *A Search for Innocence.* At this stage (which is not at all the last in time) the dramatic movement proceeds through enormous fantasies of rebellion and guilt, through waves of inhumanity, and through the savage aggressions that have always accompanied the project but are not identical with it. It becomes clear (to me) that the secular world, without eliminating one inch of my first stage, or one inch of the beauty or independence of mathematics or any other discipline or element within it, must also be imagined as place of terror and horror.

According to the intellectual convenience of the reader, the last pages of my book can be taken as part of my image of the secular project or as epilogue to that image. I have chosen to take them as epilogue. In them I try to work out the beginnings of a unifying (and differentiating) logic between the secular and the sacred. In them, above all, I propose that if the image I have given of the secular project is at all correct, if it is not only place of autonomy but also place of the human, of good and evil, of infinite search for light, and of terror, then it needs what in the first place we had given up. It needs all the resources and the separate identity of the sacred to deal with it. What will have been given up (the full identity, resources, and history of the sacred) will now return. My image will have come full circle.

ACT ONE

The Search for Man

I

The Unconditional Project

*There will be various elements or moments in our image
of secularity and the secular project. Our first element is the
unconditionality and the autonomy of the secular order. That
order needs no constitutive explanation or eternal ideas outside
of itself. This is a nonsacramental view of the world and involves
a kind of descent into hell for the religious imagination. This
first element will not suffer mutilation if it is seen as a principle
of universal redemption.*

Let our religious image of the world begin, as first but not last
moment of the image, with unconditionality. We have seen some of
the noble forms of conditionality in which the classical religious
imagination has appeared in the past and we can now call on those
forms, by their absence, to give initial light to the meaning of this
their opposite.

An imagination which has been steeped in the glories and the
beauty of conditional images and meaning is asked to do what seems
to be nothing less than put its whole history aside. This is what has
been asked of it in a definitive way since the Enlightenment. In various forms this is what is now being asked of it by a huge group of
contemporary religious activists who declare that the secular is the
sacred. I suggest: very well then, let us explore this hypothesis to the
hilt, with confidence and hope, and let us see where it leads. Where
it leads, as phase after phase of our image develops, may surprise us.

Let us imagine that we are embarking on an action, in true
Aeschylean style. The action started long ago; we have seen that it has
a background of many precursors. But now we put it on the stage in
a completely formal way to make it name itself and act itself out. The
religious imagination moves into unconditionality and autonomy. In
Scene One of this chapter I present unconditionality as idea (what

does it mean?); but in Scene Two it must abandon the pretense of being a pure idea and must become a dramatic action. The words we use today are: dramatic, dialectical, historical. From that point on to the very last phase of our image, we shall be exploring the full consequences of the image as moving image and dramatic idea. The idea already seems Promethean but this is only one of the fantasies the imagination will have to suffer through as it moves through the secular project. For Aeschylus, suffering (πάθος) is always the second phase of an imagination that is in action (δράμα).

UNCONDITIONALITY

The first factor in any image of secularity, therefore, must be autonomy and autonomous meaning; this has been at the center of all definitions of the secular world, though the image and the definition too often stopped there. Autonomy means that things do not have to go out of themselves for their meaning or reality. This does not mean that the individual fact lives in isolation and without context. But the context is its own and part of its own life. I speak therefore of a _constitutive_ autonomy. The important thing is that secularity need not seek conditions other than its own for its meaning and novelty. In this sense it is unconditional. This is my first definition of the first phase of an image of secularity. It is clearly a nonsacramental foundation for our image.

An example of the probing of the thing in itself, in its unconditional terms, is the Socratic exploration of human goodness which begins in the second book of The Republic. There it is the moral imagination that will insist on unconditionality. Socrates accepts the challenge that up to that moment in history human goodness has been judged by nothing but exterior things, by all the social profit that can come from it; it is now time, he is told, to look at the thing in itself, to isolate this good human thing, to take away every benefit from it, indeed to place the good man on the cross because of it, and then, only then, to ask if the good is still worthwhile—without any other condition save itself. This question marks an epochal human moment. The really good must be unconditional.

Here is the ironic way in which the demand for unconditionality is put by Adeimantus the great defender of conditionality. His irony is worth the space of this citation:

"Beside our picture of the unjust man let us set one of the just man, the man of true simplicity of character who, as Aeschylus says, wants 'to be and not to seem good'. We must, indeed, not allow him to seem good, for if he does he will have all the rewards and honours paid to the man who has a reputation for justice, and we shall not be able to tell whether his motive is love of justice or love of the rewards and honours. No, we must strip him of every-thing except his justice, and our picture of him must be drawn in the opposite way to our picture of the unjust man; for our just man must have the worst of reputations even though he has done no wrong. So we shall be able to test his justice and see if it can stand up to unpopularity and all that goes with it; we shall give him an undeserved and lifelong reputation for wickedness, and make him stick to his chosen course until death. In this way, when we have pushed the life of justice and of injustice each to its extreme, we shall be able to judge which of the two is the happier."

"I say, Glaucon," I put in, "you're putting the finishing touches to your two portraits as energetically as if you were getting them ready for a show."

"I'm doing my best," he said. "And these being our two characters, it is not, I think, difficult to describe the sort of life that awaits each. And if the description is somewhat crude, remember that it's not I that am responsible for it, Socrates, but those who think more of injustice than justice. It is their account that I must now repeat.

"The just man, then, as we have pictured him, will be scourged, tortured, and imprisoned, his eyes will be put out, and after enduring every humiliation he will be crucified, and learn at last that we should want not to be, but to seem just. And so that remark which I quoted from Aeschylus could be more appropriately applied to the unjust man; for he, because he deals with realities and not appearances, wants not to seem but to be unjust. He

> Reaps thought's deep furrow, for therefrom
> Spring goodly schemes."[1]

But there is a sense in which modern secularity now inundates us with such Socratic questions. Secular autonomy is not an esoteric image; it is not a theological monster, though it still causes a good deal of perturbation. Granted that autonomy often arose as the enemy of the sacred, what it can choose to be by force of its own idea is something else. What autonomy and unconditionality mean is identity and self-possession. In a truly secular world (according to my image) everything would seek and on principle be allowed to seek its own life and identity. Emergence is another good word for what I am after, particularly if emergence means the emergence of the identity of things. Secularity stands for a universal principle of emergence, of everything moving into its own and into self-possession. It wishes to communicate life to things, to people, to peoples (at this moment to Asia, Africa, Latin America), to fields of study and disciplines (biology, physics, chemistry, astronomy, medicine, music). Once again this does not mean that any fact or person or situation is closed in within its own positivistic life and is not to be defined by some broad contextual life. Nor is there any set limitation, in the sense of a final all-resolving hypothesis, to be imposed as closing-in point of the whole secular project. While the project has been traditionally fearful of *transcendental* meaning and has tried traditionally to close itself off from that problem, much of modern thought, if not its very substance, has also come to reject the closed in, noncontextual, positivistic fact. Its drive is relational and functional, and it does not establish a closing point as an ideal. This matter is so important and this distinction so difficult that I have suggested a number of good, central modern readings on the subject.[2] (These readings also indicate that modern thought is "symbolic" in a new and altogether contextual sense.)

There is no reason why this beginning of an image of secularity, based on inward life and to be thought of within the terms of secularity itself, cannot be describing a universal principle of redemption and salvation, as wide as the world in its interest and covering the wide range of history and society in a more complete image of redemption than we have been accustomed to imagine. In fact this image of universal identity is one that haunts the modern consciousness and torments it when it knows it is in the presence not of such an image but of a counter, nonhuman imitation, a fraudulent image of the secular that is defeating human life. The trouble is that once you introduce the idea of salvation into this overwhelming social and historical context, you are in great trouble as to where the point of actual redemption stands. I think it is better to say that redemption puts on a larger body. It is no longer enough to take your stand with Georges Bernanos or Graham Greene and locate redemption in some secret matters.

Unconditionality vs. Absolutism

On the other hand it would be as grievous a mistake to go beyond every measure of reasonable hope for the salvation and redemption that can come from the political and social orders of human history. There is nothing more destructive or dangerous than that human instinct which I, for one, have been in the habit of calling the absolutizing instinct and which in the present context of discussion will place no limits whatsoever on its fantasies, its enthusiasms, its hopes. Nor is it any disservice to the secular project or to any and every impulse toward advancing or reforming it, if we constantly distinguish it from its mad, imitative forms. Thus, some sectors of liberal opinion in the United States, because they did not make this distinction, misinterpreted some elements of the very distinguished work of the English historian Norman Cohn in *The Pursuit of the Millennium*, a fascinating account of those unlimited and revolutionary fanaticisms of the Middle Ages which were guided by transcendental fantasy and aimed at shattering and renewing the world. I shall take the position later and I take it now, in anticipation, that this unlimited fanaticism, this transfer of transcendental fanaticism, is one of the factors that most negates and inhibits the possibility of real movement forward in the secular order. This, I think, is also the position of Norman Cohn. For *The Pursuit of the Millennium* is not a history of revolution or of social revolt as such. We read that

> There were periods in the Middle Ages when peasant revolts and urban revolutions were very common. What is more, these insurrections of the common people stood them in excellent stead, compelling concessions, bringing solid gains in prosperity and privilege. In the age-old laborious struggle against oppression and exploita-

tion, the peasants and artisans of medieval Europe played no ignoble part. But the movements described in this book are in no way typical of the efforts which the poor made to improve their lot. Rather, they constitute a special type of social movement—a relatively rare type, but not the less significant for that. *Prophetae* would construct their apocalyptic lore out of the most varied materials—the Book of Daniel, the Book of Revelation, the Sibylline Oracles, the speculations of Joachim of Fiore, the doctrine of the Equalitarian State of Nature—all of them elaborated, and reinterpreted and vulgarized. That lore would be purveyed to the masses—and the result would be something which was at once a revolutionary movement and an outburst of quasi-religious salvationism.[3]

There have been many wild and daimonic forces that have sought or promised complete and absolute salvation in the secular project. Such forces represent one significant part of those elements that introduce the factor of terror and horror into the secular world. These forces are always helped by actual or impending disaster. Perhaps it is because they rush into a vacuum of hopelessness with a bright, overwhelming dream that must be executed immediately without paying attention to the human and earthbound rhythms of Aeschylus: drama and pathos and learning. There were the plagues that prefaced the First Crusade and the flagellant movements of 1260, 1348–49, 1391, and 1400; there were the famines that signaled the First and Second Crusades. "The greatest wave of Chiliastic excitement, one which swept through the whole of society, was precipitated by the most universal natural disaster of the Middle Ages, the Black Death."[4] The religious imagination cannot accept this absolutizing image of the secular world. But it must be able to deal with the terror and the evils these absolutes create in the secular world. Blessed is the nation that needs no messiah.

At any rate these fantastic worlds are endlessly removed from the unconditional existence that is the subject of this chapter.

For one thing, there is nothing that requires more discipline than the kind of unconditionality we have been talking about, and there is nothing that has as many spurious imitations of itself. It requires constant discipline of the mind and of egotistic instincts to give life and motivation to a thing and not take it away, to insist that any one thing or person or situation or problem is not another. It took thousands of years before civilization could reach the point of asking the question put by Socrates. That question—and all early questions like it—is thought by many to be the origin of modern science and objectivity.

But this unconditionality has many substitutes, some of them superficially magnificent. Much so-called unconditional thinking among us is supremely conditional. Very much of our social thinking emanates from package deals which describe the images of culture gangs and culture warfare among us at this moment. The polarized images of the Left and the Right, the liberals and the conservatives, are very often not fixed at all on the good of the unconditional thing in itself but on the thing in itself as a condition of striking at the other group. The polarized imagination is a highly conditioned imagination; it is not interested in the truth. It is ironic that the Left and the Right are so preoccupied with each other precisely at a time when the imaginations of both have become less and less concerned with the world, with the vast undeveloped world of Asia, Africa, Latin-America—where surely the most decisive questions of identity and emergence stare us in the face for the future. A devotion to this vast field of unconditionality would help drive us out of many of those regions of thought and feeling which are presently conditioned to the point of hysteria. It is hard to see how so elemental a decision can be missed. The ultimate crisis in the modern secular project will be the enormous and growing difference between the rich and the poor nations. How can the development of life and the emergence of man in the undeveloped continents not be fundamental? At any rate, it should be clear how difficult a spirituality is necessary if we are to have a civilization that is truly based on unconditionality.

There are two things that must be kept together if we are to read this first unconditional phase of an image of the secular correctly. The two things are the modern sense of the unconditional finite and the modern sense of the infinite. Whatever number man now names he knows there is an infinite number beyond it. Whatever step he takes he knows that it is one of an infinite number of alternatives; it is also only a dent in an infinite that still remains for exploration.[5] With every human statement there is also a statement of an open world, but the human limited statement is no longer an imitation of or participation in a transcendent, infinite world; in its inner, constitutive life it is an absolute and does not go looking in an infinite light or dark for a legitimization of itself. *The infinite is a perspective but never a confirmation or a higher substitute.* Fantasy will immediately say that this is an abandonment of law, norm, idea, morality; as a matter of fact it involves a closer examination of the truth. For our truth is human and can be found nowhere else. I will propose later that God put on our mind in making the world. Therefore the center of meaning always remains the unconditional, human fact.

One reaction to this image of pure unconditionality has been that it involves an image of absurdity. But why? I walk out into the street and see exactly what is there: a few houses, attractive or dull; a few people who happened to be there; a little rain or sunshine; I hear a sudden small noise. I am told that if it is sheer unconditionality, unsupported by an eternal idea, it is absurd and that it should drive me to suicide. I read *The Waste Land* and am told that it is all very bad. I see the films of Antonioni and am told that it is even worse. I know that things are very bad but not for the usual conventional reasons of the unconventional people. If we can get to the point where we can readily ask the question "but why?"—then we will have removed extraordinary burdens from an imagination that seeks to establish endless conditions for looking at anything or doing anything. My question in this book is: Can we simplify this burden and establish secular unconditionality in religious terms?

What secularity objects to is the precondition that predetermines and forecloses. Is it from Gide that Jean-Paul Sartre has learned his own analysis of the authentic and the inauthentic, the criticism of the type of mind (*salaud*) that will fall back on an alleged principle to avoid fidelity to a given fact. The central difficulty with Sartre is that he is possessed of a huge a priori of his own which enters into all experience for him, no matter how much he claims he has purified that experience of every condition or interpretation or defense save that of existence. It is the great a priori of nausea. I make my own calculation about the origin of this disgust. It is that there is a strange fellowship here on the part of Sartre and on the part of the overburdened religious imagination. Both walk into the street to look at scenes I have mentioned, and at chairs, desks, roots of trees, anything at all—

the one with all the expectations of a world charged with religious symbol, the other with all the expectations of the infinitely rationalizing mind—and both are disappointed.

But, I keep asking the question, why *should* they be? What did they expect? Why can neither accept unconditionality? The first need of the imagination is to desymbolize or "decreate" (this is a word I have taken from Frank Kermode[6] who, in turn, has taken it from Simone Weil). This quest of the autonomy and unconditionality of the world is in the air in many nonreligious forms.

The aspiration toward an unconditional image in things may be the largest factor behind the increasing hostility to metaphysics in our time. What is really at stake is hostility to a long history of finding the meaning of the literal things in front of us *outside*, in the form of double and external images of themselves. There is a general effort to de-pack or desymbolize our images of the world—an effort to start with their unconditionality. We have been experiencing a general attack on every form of two-world theory which insists that nothing has meaning unless it has a counterpart outside of itself in another world. This may explain our interest in Happenings and in Fragments.

It is not necessary to conclude that we are in the midst of a crude revival of nominalism, a dedication to the single concrete thing, a rejection of meaning and universals.

There are a number of ways the arts have found as their way of expressing this modern passion for unconditionality. All of them are fascinating and a great help to the understanding as long as we do not isolate any one of them and declare that this and precisely this is that noble thing called unconditionality with which we begin our own voyage of image making.

There is the attraction among us for the truth and the strength of the irreducible image, impervious to analyses or explanation, and presenting reality as nakedly *there*. If we combine with this kind of unconditionality the endless series of attacks on form that have characterized what we came to call modernism we come to endless manifestations and symbols, good and bad, of the wish to get underneath every unnecessary condition, explanation, form, frame, institution, of existence and life itself. Every measure was being resorted to to get at unconditionality. Some of the measures were profound, others inevitably a mere game, full of the very inauthenticity they denounced. We have had the experience of a passionate attack on words in the arts and on anything resembling interpretation. In the theater it became almost forbidden to talk about the form of an action. And I have called attention to how much unmasking of things and people has been going on. Again for good or for bad everybody has been taking masks off everybody else; everybody wishes to get below the surface. What has been happening has been a bold metaphysical search for a less conditioned reality, accompanied by all kinds of cheap imitations of the real metaphysical quest. That is always the case.

Within these terms of unconditionality I think we also have begun to discuss something quite central for the whole understanding of contemporary faith. We have seen that the consciousness of the religious man is now torn into two separated parts. One part is idealistic and filled with a passion for religious meaning; the other part is secular, pragmatic, and full of the spirit of unconditionality. The first part is still not at home in a modern scene, and that is not because the architecture and television are so bad. Thus a split consciousness in the religious imagination. It is full of dreams and double images. What it needs is a movement toward realism, toward a realistic faith that spends less time in tormenting the human spirit about secularity than in dealing with unconditionality. I have called this a "descent into hell" on the part of this idealistic faith, but my hope is that we are already part of the way up by the very fact of having named the problem. And I think we are on a path that is called for by the final logic of religious thought itself.

One thing the religious imagination must face, I repeat, is that the religious symbol is no help in understanding the type of unconditionality that is the mark of secularism. Here I shall ask the patience of waiting for the end of this book before my own total view of the future life of the religious and Christian symbol breaks back in a different way into the light. All that I am saying at this stage is that no understanding of and no contribution to unconditional secularity is reached by imposing religious symbols upon its content or forms. This is especially true of the now enormous content of the modern sciences and of all those disciplines and fields which are specifically secular.

UNCONDITIONALITY OF THE IMAGINATION

May I say that I have been trying to explore the problem of freedom and innocence and the unconditional life on the double level of the self and the world, the microcosm and the macrocosm. In an earlier book, on hope,[7] I tried to sketch a path of approximation to innocence for the mentally ill. There it was a matter of taking away from the sick the burden of finding a one, nonexistent *right* way in all situations, an inscrutable way of the will of God, that would come from outside our own wishes and would condition all of these wishes. There is no greater torment than this kind of endless, external search for innocence. We must restore the primacy of man as a wishing being who, as long as he is within reality, creates the right thing by the absolute unconditionality of his own wishing. The wish does not have to go out of itself. . . . But now, in the construction of this new image, we make the same experiment for secularity. If there is an unconditionality of the human wish, so too there is an unconditionality of the human imagination. There is an inner all-rightness of things as they are and as I see them, in their own identity, without going out of themselves. Again, what the first search sought for was an equation between unconditional wishing and innocence. Now we look for an equation between innocence and the marvelous unconditionality of secularity.

Finally, for whatever the reason, secular unconditionality seems to be an image of reality that is more easily digested by the imagination of Protestant theologians than by Catholics. There is a tradition of the secular image in Protestantism and there is a tradition of the sacramental and Christic image in Catholicism. I think that this has been a root cause of division that has not been sufficiently discussed. The Catholic imagination has not been happy in this state of unconditionality and tends much more to seek the final sacramental view. On the other hand Protestantism has not always accepted the secular image for the right reasons.

It is a fact that the image of the world as secularized has become more native to the Reformation and Protestantism. Let me give a few brief examples. Carl Michalson in his *Worldly Theology* thinks of the Reformation as the only major attempt to reintroduce the meaning of the Christian movement as the secularizing of the world.[8]

William O. Fennell, in an essay called "The Theology of the Secularity," does not hesitate about our unconditional center of the secular image. It would be hard to speak more firmly about the point:

> The doctrine of the world we feel constrained to call into question . . . is that which thinks to find the world's true being and meaning in its transparency to God. Such a religious, sacramentalist view of nature seems to do justice neither to the nature of God, nor to the nature of the world. These are made known in the historical self-manifestation of God to which the Scriptures bear witness. . . . It does not do justice to God who is self-revealed as one whose gracious will it is to create and to redeem, not for his own but for the being and the good of another than himself. . . . he sets it [the world] free from himself to be itself.[9]

There are two books by Ronald Gregor Smith, *The New Man* and *Secular Christianity*,[10] which contain a strong criticism of every attempt of metaphysical (and theological) systems to be restraining conditions for that freedom and manifoldness of the new reality which have made it impossible that either philosophy or theology reign any longer as queens of the sciences. History is no longer to be thought of as a "tiresome ante-chamber of supra-history," but as a power whose meaning could be found in itself.[11] As others do, he attributes his own positive view of secularity to the German theologian Friedrich Gogarten, in his *Verhängnis und Hoffnung der Neuzeit Säkularisierung als Theologisches Problem*. Gogarten is one of the principal modern heroes of the secular image of the world (and he traces his view back to Luther).[12]

What is interesting here is the inclination of some of the Protestant theologians to locate this confidence (in the simple unconditionality of the secular world) in the area of faith. According to this way of thinking there is the act of faith in God but there is also a fundamental faith in the reality of the whole world. Thus Schubert Ogden in his latest book *The Reality of God*,[13] as well as Van Harvey in *The Historian and the Believer*.[14]

The fervent defense of secularity by some Protestant images is rooted in a dialectical theology which comes to a nonsacramental view of the world because of the absolute and radical abyss between God and the world. I want to get to the same nonsacramental and unconditional goal, but I have already expressed my great distrust of some dialectical ways of getting there. I shall propose my own and different dialectic in this book. But now let me say just one thing in simple summary. I am clearly proposing that the Catholic image must pass through severe changes (Karl Rahner, John Metz and others are helping toward that change), but that will not mean that all the Protestant images of the secular must be accepted as adequate, especially those of a dialectical or existential character.

Perhaps the divisions and the misunderstandings will grow less as we move into the dramatic stage and the permanently dramatic state of our image of the secular project. The unconditionality that has been reached must be kept as a permanent achievement, undiluted, making much of our civilization possible. But we must not decide that we are now bogged down in bare facts, in naked existence, in pure experience, in unadulterated images that must at all cost be without interpretation. All that would only leave us back with Francis Bacon and his pure facts, though in a more sophisticated mode of language. The secular project has given up that view of itself and its world of unconditionality.

In our next scene the pure idea will become dramatic idea or image.

II

The Human Project

The unconditionality of the secular project cannot remain a pure idea. It must become a dramatic image. It must pass from secular project to human project. The purely cosmocentric image of life must pass into an anthropocentric image, with man at the center once more. We discover the unconditionality of

the human imagination over against the unconditionality, the
Prometheanism, of the will. Our image must pass not through a
part but through the whole of the human.

We come then to the next stage of our image, a new moment in
which the image of secularity must become dramatic. It must pass out
of the stage of being a simple, innocent, and pure idea of unconditionality. It must begin to pass through every manner of counterimage of
itself, in order to become itself. (But to pass through a counterimage
is not to pass through a double image.)

The first moment of this attempt at a new image has set out on
a new action, in imitation of Aeschylean style. It sets out on its own
unconditional life, choosing to cross the gap from conditionality into
absolute unconditionality and independence. It refuses to be the
double of anything. It refuses to find its own meaning in another
world of forms which is a more solemn double of itself. It has an
adventurous spirit which cannot allow itself to be defined in terms of
being a mere illustration or doublement of something else already
accomplished. It is new in every way, and does not see that that involves hostility in any way. This involves the rejection of many "dou-
bling" forms of metaphysics and a setting out on a more open path.

But a simple unconditional image of secularity, thus far constructed, is a pure abstraction. The reality involves a difficult and painful, a dramatic and dialectical process. Any other image is abstract and
naïve. It is not an idea that some have and others do not. It is not an
idea that the intellectuals have and others alas do not; or that the
young have and others do not; or that one class has and another does
not. The secular project is dramatic and dialectical everywhere, at its
very heart. In this sense there is always a double image. For the idea
is always in the presence of its opposite and corrupted forms: injustice, the concentration of wealth, bureaucracy, contempt of the spirit
and of identity, righteousness, hatred, suffering. It is always facing
and mastering imitations of itself. But revolutionary withdrawal into
the pure idea is absurd.

If we admit that there is a pure Cartesian, nondramatic image
of secularity, in all its beauty and innocence, someone will always
come along to claim that he has it. This book is in part about a search
for innocence on the part of secularity; but innocence is not only a

beautiful goal; it is also a very dangerous one. Once you have absolute innocence, you find it is possessed of projective powers which in hatred cast *all* guilt upon the dehumanized image of some other group.[15] Thus the greatest enemy of the real moral energy and earnestness of the new generation is a too facile innocence. An innocence that is not come by the hard way will lead to the violences of innocence. There is nothing more violent than this kind of purity.

The secular image as *dramatic* means that it is a difficult, positive, and magnificent ideal of universal identity and unconditionality which can only become itself by passing through and purifying itself from the ugly reality of its opposites. The irony is that the very secularity whose vocation is to create identity is itself never free of the problem of confused identity. The project *is* innocent but it seems necessary to find this out the hard dramatic way.

THE ANTHROPOCENTRIC VS. THE COSMOCENTRIC

The central dramatic fact is the passage of the secular project from a cosmocentric to an anthropocentric structure. I am going to re-present this passage with the help of Promethean figures old and new.

One must imagine the project not as passing through endless space and ambition but as passing *through the human and through all of the human.* The unconditionality of the world, talked about so objectively in our previous scene, must now become the unconditionality of man.

All the things in man's world are not good unless they are human and submitted to the laws of a human being. They must move through man. They have no unconditional or autonomous stage before they encounter man. The laws of economics and politics must be his laws, the laws of the human. There are no eternal laws of economics or politics to which he must submit, whether they be human or no. It cannot be said to him, though it is, that business is business and he must face it; or politics are politics and he must swallow it all; or war is war, with its own laws, and he must face all these things as though they were eternal laws of being and God. By the same token he cannot be told that modernization is modernization, with its own absolute, unconditional, and sacrosanct laws.

It is here, in these areas of life that have become self-enclosed and independent of the human, that true secularity is meeting its worst contemporary crisis. For true secularity should not try to defend its unconditionality against the human. But its counterimages, its parody forms, do try; the most notorious independent form is *technique*. I define the word, not according to any sensible use the world makes of method, nor according to any limited version of technique, nor according to its relation to the machine, but according to the universal sense given to the word by Jacques Ellul in his provocative book *The Technological Society*:

> The term Technique, as I use it, does not mean machines, technology, or this or that procedure for attaining an end. In our technological society, *technique is the totality of methods rationally arrived at* and having absolute efficiency (for a given stage of development) in every field of human activity. Its characteristics are new; the technique of the present has no common measure with that of the past.[16]

The Technique of the present wishes to become total.

Technique as a universal, interacting, self-escalating creator of a worldwide spirituality of efficient means independent of ends is our concern. It is an endless process if it does not confront itself with the human.

Thus we quickly find ourselves in the middle of the difference between the cosmocentric and the anthropocentric. What is the difference?

According to an anthropocentric point of view, man would be at the center once more, and the earth with him, as they were before the days of Copernicus, though in new senses of being at the center. The older religious image of man was what we might call cosmocentric; now a great part of its life must become anthropocentric. I shall give geometrical images of these two words.

The religious imagination has often inclined to live in a completely cosmocentric point of view and with a cosmocentric set of images. It has imagined itself and man as a *point* in the cosmos which moves through the tremendous area of all the other points in order to get somewhere, whether it uses them as a ladder on which to rise, or as means to an end, or as objects to contemplate as well as to transcend.

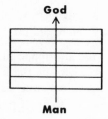

We have also called it *the* religious world or point of view and that, if inflexibly held to, is a mistake, because it will limit the whole life of the religious imagination. The latter can never abandon the cosmos or being or God as center, but it also possesses enormous resources to help the world construct that which religion unnecessarily fears, an anthropocentric world, with man and the human also as center and measure of all things. Let us fumble for a first image of the way such a world would look.

The way it looks is that first it reverses the cosmocentric image, so that all things in the cosmos (C) are moving through man as a ladder or, at any rate, as a center.

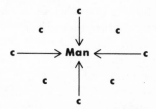

This view seems to declare that God and being are no longer the center if man is; worse still, it seems to imply a vast hostility and to re-create all the fantasies of Prometheus on an even greater scale than that conjectured by the imagination of Aeschylus. They might be the fantasies that surged up in the heart of the Prometheus of Goethe:

> Here I sit, shaping man
> After my image,

A race that is like me,
To suffer, to weep,
To rejoice and be glad,
And like myself
To have no regard for you![17]

The relation between the anthropocentric and the cosmocentric is the central problem. It will become the final problem of this book and of the image it is trying to construct. The problem of this relationship has finally taken on the sharpest possible terms. What is the relation of human interiority to the outside world? There are vast waves of feeling among us that do not hesitate to characterize every version of the outside and of otherness as enemy. Among the great progenitors of this point of view, which freezes the relationship, are Hegel, Goethe, and Kierkegaard. The image is again hardening at our moment of history. The outside is often enemy to interiority. The world is enemy. There is a warfare going on between me and the world.

PROMETHEUS VS. PROMETHEANISM

I begin by making a distinction between Prometheus and Prometheanism. We may find that we have badly distorted the meaning of the original Prometheus and that what we might need in our day is the emergence of many another Prometheus.

Is it too much to say that all the difficulties with the corrupt part of the history of secularity have come from an overly simplistic image of the human and of movement through the human? It is the disease of the imagination called simplicism which has driven the secular project into that worst of all its deformities called Prometheanism. For the Prometheanism which we have often associated with the image of secularity itself is a rigid, simplistic, unilinear image of movement through the human, based on power and the will and ultimately involving a lack of imagination. It is an image of power, victory, invention, engineering, unilinear progress, and unilinear evolution, the conquest of the world. In short it has meant and still means a unilinear and distorting image of man's relation to the outside world. We can only be redeemed from it by a more diverse, a more analogical image of human movement and of movement through things human. We must imagine human movement not only in heroic terms but after the manner of a prism with uncountable faces. We must beware of the men of one idea. There are more forms of movement than by straight lines. The secular project must explore the total movement of human sensibility. This will also mean an exploration of the image of tragedy. How otherwise could the project include the poor, the dumb, the nonbeautiful. It must not be a project of the beautiful people.

This scene, therefore, begins to imagine a secular project that is totally human. It is largely an analysis of that caricature of secularity that we find in Prometheanism.

The myth of Prometheus was a first great milestone in dealing with the most fundamental of all the questions that have plagued the relations between the sacred and the secular: Can man have his own free movement and life according to his own resources and with his own ends, in any kind of independence of religion, God, the sacred? (The god who helped chain Prometheus to a Caucasian mountain fastness because he had brought fire and the arts to man declares: "Zeus alone is free.") This has remained an abiding question in theology. In our own day it has again become a central question of our own contemporary theologizing: Has man come alive; is God dead? The same question of autonomous action is debated at the very center of the soul of the modern artist as he seeks freedom from "reality." All in all the question has never been more intensely asked than in our own time. But the question of Prometheus is too often reduced to the question of Prometheanism.

I will not review the long history of the myth and metaphor of Prometheus (there is an excellent account of its literary history in Raymond Trousson's two-volume Le Thème de Prométhée dans la litterature Européenne).[18] But let me stay for a little while with some of its absorbing images.

Among the many myths and symbols under which the world began to think of "secularity" (though the present range of the word would have frightened the ancients) that of Prometheus might well rank first. So central and universal is the place of fire in the growth of human civilization and resource that it is impossible to locate any first ethnic or geographic origin for the story of the man or Titan or god who first gave it to us. There is the equivalent of the Prometheus legend everywhere. It is Hesiod who was the initiator of the story among the Greeks, but the story as told by him is rough and unsophisticated: Prometheus is the Evil One who is rightly punished by Zeus for giving fire to man, and Zeus rightly sends woman—Athena—upon man as a punishing scourge for such a crime! It may have been partly in anti-Hesiodic protest that Aeschylus composed the incomparable version which has been the precursor of a long line of literary explorations of the theme. It is in the Aeschylean Prometheus that this divine fire becomes the concrete image of civilization itself. There is the simple sentence of Werner Jaeger: "Prometheus was the civilising genius who explores the whole world, who makes it subservient to his will by organizing its forces, who reveals its treasures and establishes on a firm basis the groping insecure life of man."[19] And it was the literary and theological genius of Aeschylus that first seized the dimensions of the word *Prometheus* as symbol of the quarrel between the autonomy of God and the autonomy of man.

It is not possible to understand what Aeschylus is doing in the *Prometheus Bound* unless we recur to the fact that we are dealing with a dramatic way of thinking and imagining. I have followed that method as completely as possible in constructing my own image of secularity, but it is from men like Aeschylus that we learn the method. I fervently wish, in the fever for the dehellenization of Christianity that is again going on among the theologians, that they would stop their obsessive reduction of all Greek thought to "essentialism" and would discover the intense and universal dramatic genius of the Greeks. An example would be the present case of Aeschylus. What was he doing in the *Prometheus Bound?* To use that terrible word, what was his *method* in dealing with his idea of Prometheanism?

The question could be asked in this form: How could the profoundly religious soul of Aeschylus have written such a play, in which the fire, anger, resentment, and rebellion of man on the one hand and the dubious and punitive justice of a primitive Zeus on the other are among the more lasting impressions? Does it not seem that Prometheus comes off better than God? True, the play is much more complicated than its ordinary reputation, as are its feelings on both the secular and the sacred side. It is among the last and not the earlier works of Aeschylus. And it is a more involved, a more sophisticated version of the battle of man with God than are the Prometheus versions of writers of the stature of Goethe or Shelley or Byron. But after all this has been remembered, it is still plausible to give it the simple reading of an antireligious attack upon Zeus; it is because it is often so understood by so many later Promethean composers that it has helped create the later narrow crudity of the human imagination called Prometheanism.

But if the play is understood in these simplistic terms, and if it has helped to fashion the human simplicism called Prometheanism, it is because it is neither read nor understood dramatically.

A dramatic idea gets said totally, in its entire history of feeling and action, in all its parts. The contemporary quarrel about the nature of drama and our restless exploration into new forms need not confuse what we are trying to say here. What was happening with Prometheus? So far as he was concerned he was refusing to abandon man to the anger of God and was helping him to take his first great steps by human resource into the endless dark. But this means venturing on the path of freedom, whereas Kratos has pronounced that "none is free but Zeus." It meant rebellion against this dictum. Perhaps it meant interpreting all the terrible adversities of the world, the wind, the rain, the inner and outer storm and death, as punishment for man's invading the impassable ditch that destiny had set up between man and God.

It seems altogether right, therefore, that the very first Aeschylean scene should represent the absolute domination of Zeus and of the mighty cosmocentric forces of the world that are set against men and against Prometheus, their champion. Hard, stern images represent the first stages of the action, the beginning of man's search for a human life: Hephaestus is the only kind voice; Might and Violence are performing their dreadful tasks; the autonomy of Zeus is absolute and unshared; Prometheus is not only separated from God; it is important to note how separated he also is, as the action begins, from humanity and the consolations of all things truly human. There is the great paradigm of the secular problem from the very beginning—Prometheus initiates the freedom and advance of man, and then begins to suffer:

SCENE: A bare and desolate crag in the Caucasus. Enter Might and
Violence, demons, servants of Zeus, and Hephaestus, the
smith.

Might

This is world's limit that we have come to; this is the Scythian
country, an untrodden desolation. Hephaestus, it is you that
must heed the commands the Father laid upon you to nail this
malefactor to the high craggy rocks in fetters unbreakable of
adamantine chain. For it was your flower, the brightness of fire
that devises all, that he stole and gave to mortal men; this is the
sin for which he must pay the Gods the penalty—that he may
learn to endure and like the sovereignty of Zeus and quit his
man-loving disposition.

Hephaestus

. . . High-contriving Son of Themis of Straight Counsel: this is
not of your will nor of mine; yet I shall nail you in bonds of
indissoluble bronze on this crag far from men. Here you shall
hear no voice of mortal; here you shall see no form of mortal.
You shall be grilled by the sun's bright fire and change the fair
bloom of your skin. You shall be glad when Night comes with
her mantle of stars and hides the sun's light; but the sun shall
scatter the hoarfrost again at dawn. Always the grievous burden
of your torture will be there to wear you down; for he that shall
cause it to cease has yet to be born. . . .

Might

Come, why are you holding back? Why are you pitying in vain?
Why is it that you do not hate a God whom the Gods hate most
of all? Why do you not hate him, since it was your honor that he
betrayed to men?

Hephaestus

Our kinship has strange power; that, and our life together.

Might

Yes. But to turn a deaf ear to the Father's words—how can that
be? Do you not fear that more?

Hephaestus
You are always pitiless, always full of ruthlessness.

Might
There is no good singing dirges over him. Do not labor uselessly at what helps not at all.

Hephaestus
O handicraft of mine—that I deeply hate!

Might
Why do you hate it? To speak simply, your craft is in no way the author of his present troubles.

Hephaestus
Yet would another had had this craft allotted to him.

Might
There is nothing without discomfort except the overlordship of the Gods. For only Zeus is free.

Hephaestus
I know. I have no answer to this.[20]

Hephaestus has no answer, but ever since we have been seeking an answer to this awesome domination and cosmocentric loneliness of the universe. There has been a dramatic beginning of human resource and assertion. But it has no sooner begun than it is the cause of a strange crisis of suffering, alienation, punishment.

There is anger and bitterness on both sides. After the stealing of fire Prometheus had pushed on and become the teacher of all the arts to men. He alone had taken the side of man against divine anger and its threat to destroy the whole race ("these things none sought to withstand save me"). Those who before had been like helpless children in the face of the world he then made thoughtful and full of wit. He taught them through carpentry to build houses. He gave them judgment to read the rising and the setting of the stars, to put letters together into a language, to yoke beasts to their service, to build ships that would master the sea, to make food, drink, and medicine. What harm in this? But the air is full of double fantasy, that of the secular and the sacred, of Prometheus and Zeus, from the beginning. In some strange way man is branded guilty for his secularity, and he responds, not only with guilt, but with rebellion, defiance, a refusal to submit to the world's injustice. Zeus interprets things in his own way, according to mathematical justice and strict definitions of the difference between the human and the divine. The *Prometheus Bound* begins and ends in rebellious torture, in loneliness, agony, defiance, and finally, under the thunderbolt, on a Caucasian mountain fastness. But we often interpret that against such a God, Prometheus is the real victor.

Something like this is what actually must have happened, had to happen, between secular and sacred, man and God, the anthropocentric and the cosmocentric. All these events (and feelings) were in some fashion there (and still are). Aeschylus lets them come out, as the feelings and facts of man versus the world. The important thing is that they are also our feelings. The first step must be a dramatic liberation of the realities and feelings that are there and that must be dealt with, especially the cries of injustice against the world, the cries of rightful human wishes, the place of human resources, but also the groan of unnameable guilt. This is what the imagination must move through. We still move through it, and though our drama is different we still dramatize it all. There is the same cry at the end of the *Three Sisters* of Chekhov.

In Aeschylus both the problem of secularity and the true task of the dramatic imagination come into their own together. Especially in *Works and Days* Hesiod had reduced Prometheus to the status of a bad example of a good moral principle, an example of a bad boy who has not obeyed the gods and has thus brought many woes on the human race. But in Aeschylus the imagination literally moves through the whole experience of Prometheus, inward and outward; it searches for the dimensions of the problem; it gathers insights as it moves. It is aware that the problem still exists, and that it is moving through its own human and theological life. Aeschylus allows the movement toward understanding and solution to occur on every level, human and divine. For there was a sequel (*Prometheus Unbound*) and possibly a third play, in which both man and God have moved forward toward light, growth, and reconciliation. They will have abandoned their original tragic and rigid statement of the case against each other.

It would not be too much to say that a chief quality of the dramatic imagination in all the plays of Aeschylus (with the possible exception of the *Seven Against Thebes*) is a progressive refinement of movement as the playwright moves through original rigidities toward a wider and reconciling image. I shall have occasion later to return to this special gift of his in the *Oresteia*. The imagination of Aeschylus does not get *stuck*, and the *Prometheus* plays did not get stuck in Prometheanism. The rigidity and unilinear power of Prometheanism could learn much from *this* Prometheus.

I do not know what we have to learn from the Prometheus of Goethe, which set such a guidepost for the interiorizing, divinized spirit of Promethean creativity that it finally frightened even Goethe himself. I doubt too that we now have anything to learn from the masterpiece of Shelley. It is too lyrically hopeful an expression of Prometheanism, too close to the romantic dreams that followed the French Revolution to miss filling us today with cynicism. Byron's *Manfred*, despite the staginess of its characters and unimaginable solemnity of its crucial images, comes off most modernly for me as an account of where we stand, within and without, as a new and latest Promethean band. It is as frightened as we are by the sense of the surrounding infinite; as for our alienation, it breaks out in one great continuing metaphor in the soul of Manfred; as for the search for innocence, Shelley does not even know what guilt is, but Byron is completely overwhelmed. *Manfred* is more a *Faustus* than a *Prometheus*, but it has been under the enormous influence of the hero of Aeschylus and it has the Aeschylean sense of the suffering that always goes into the secular project.

Unconditional Imagination vs. Unconditional Will

Today we do not go about writing Promethean plays but there was never more interest in the study of the stark human will as it tends to get separated from the imagination and the rest of the human reality. In fact this would be as good a definition as any for the type of Prometheanism we are trying in this section to expunge from our image of the secular project: Prometheanism is the project of a will separated from the imagination and from reality, separated, therefore from most of the human. If I should borrow another language, this time from Allen Tate speaking of Edgar Allen Poe as a cousin of us all, Prometheanism is a world of sensation but it is not a world of large human *sensibility*. This distinction is fundamental. The pure sensation of power is a cheap imitation of sensibility.

We come to the dramatic method of image and counterimage, the passage of image through counterimage in order to become itself. Now, however, the terms of the passage are becoming more complicated. The image is secularity and at this point the counterimage is Prometheanism; the image is imagination itself and the counterimage is all the forms of the will and power which seek to imitate the task of the imagination as the latter tries to bring identity to everything human; above all, the image of unconditionality with which we began is in a struggle with a counterimage which I shall call the unconditionality of the will and of Prometheanism. Let us compare the unconditionality of the imagination with that of the will.

The greatest vocation of the imagination, as Martin Buber says, is to imagine reality, whether by finding or making it. We then add that we will never be able to exhaust the forms of this movement, but it must never be allowed to become unilinear. The important thing is that it is in a search for the unconditionality of things, but never without a struggle. It is in a search for the identifying, redeeming shape, nature, movement, history, and relations of things. It cannot tolerate single, mechanical ideas that ignore, blur, distort, or destroy these things. This is particularly true for human beings and for everything that is human. The imagination is a search, both wide and multiple, for the unconditionality of the world, and now there is no reason why we should not equate the task of secularity and that of the imagination.

But if secularity has its counterfeits, so does the imagination and so does unconditionality. When the will (and Prometheanism) separates itself from the imagination it is in order to institute a search for a fraudulent brand of unconditionality. *I define the terms of such an unconditionality of power in this simple way, that nothing must get in its way; there must be no conditions. But I again define the unconditionality of secularity as that which has no conditions outside of its own unconditional self; it is its own condition but condition indeed.* This must be seen as a startling difference. Thus there was a secret Prometheanism running through the symbolist poetry of the late nineteenth century wherever it found and declared that the actual density of things, the actual condition of things, was a block to, and an enemy of, the imagination. (The actual rose was a block to the perfect rose.) Its own unconditionality (its search for the absolute) could not handle or tolerate the unconditionality of the world. Things were simply in the way. As far as was possible, the refractory nature of reality had to be eliminated. Prometheanism handles the refractory nature of human beings in the same way. In Prometheanism the unconditionality of the will cannot accept the unconditionality of the imagination. There is a war between unconditionalities.

The Promethean imagination (and its unconditionality) is only imitating the real imagination (and its unconditionality). At all costs, it must announce to itself that it is imagining (for who can afford to admit that he is not imagining?), but it has a secret hatred of the truly human imagination and its brand of unconditionality.

The Promethean imagination has many forms.

It is like a very sick joke that cannot stand the boundaries of the really funny but must break out of it beyond the funny. Or it must always be, hysterically, a pitch above the evidence. Or because it dare not imagine death, it gesticulates wildly and imitates the imagining of death by death's pornographic form of violence. Or again and again it resorts to a magnificence that always misses the true and smaller lines of the human. Or because it cannot imagine its own evil it resorts to the larger and larger fantasy of a scapegoat. (Our present atmosphere is full of scapegoats and imagined devils). Or being never quite sure of what it is doing, it must be more certain about everything than everybody else; it will therefore invent all kinds of slogans which will be another imitation of the imagination. It imposes its own unconditionality upon the unconditionality of the imagination, and thereby destroys the imagination. But it has to find a substitute. Prometheanism itself is such a substitute, a substitute whose success depends on sounding, noisily or efficiently, like the real thing. Because it has no patience with the unconditional and therefore refractory quality of things or with their reality, their struggle and their identities, its own inner life is marked by frightening forms of endlessness, a movement without end or form or object or pause. Its unconditionality takes the form of endlessness. I shall explore that quality at length in the following chapter.

If the human imagination has its own version of the cosmological problem, so too does the intelligence. This is a delicate question, which desperately needs the right mode of expression, but that is no final reason why we should not pick up our courage and ask it. The question could be put in this form: Does the human intelligence, does Prometheus, have the right to think any and every thought? Can the intelligence lead a freewheeling existence apart from the human? Does it have its own absolutely free and independent space and cosmos and life? It is almost impossible to find a language to ask these questions that will not have political or moral overtones, even dangerous overtones so far as it might affect every magnificent ideal we have of intellectual liberty. But let us go ahead and take some risks. It was the intellectual, not the politician, who thought of the hydrogen bomb, and we know that he does feel guilty. But this is only a classical, super-instance of the cosmological independence of the intelligence. It was the intellect and the intellectual, thinking in sheer space and not humanly, who had the thought of the assembly line. It is the intellectual who formed all the complicated images of our complicated world, for good and bad. Most of our Systems were born in his head. Our future systems and all the possibilities of man as increasingly open idea, physically, biologically, psychologically, are now being conceived in the same place. There are very many forces that have produced and will produce these effects; all I am saying is that one of them has been and will be the freewheeling intelligence, dancing in infinite space, its own space, with no law but its own. The rest of the human is frightened at this new cosmos. (It is still another return of the cosmological). But the best enemy of all this must be, not authority, not any outside force, but the intelligence itself, leading its own dramatic life, at odds with its own counter and nonhuman images.

These are some of the issues that arise as humanity tries to move into a more totally human image of secularity. We must understand, and especially the religious imagination must understand, that the focus of the dilemma of the secular project has shifted a very great deal since the time of the first Prometheus as he was imagined by Aeschylus. Then the sole direction of the secular dilemma was the absolute unconditionality of Zeus and the sacred: for "Zeus alone is free." I have suggested in the Prologue that the question "how then could man be free, how then could there be a human unconditional?"

was the central theological issue from Aeschylus to the end of the Middle Ages. This is no longer the true focus of the dilemma even for the religious imagination. It would now better read: How can human unconditionality win the day against the world of objects, the world of the will, the world of the pure idea? This should not only be the secular question, it should also be the religious question. This is the new form of human self-assertion and salvation. The question is not the death of God. Such a discussion is only a disguise for the real issue.

THE MODERN PROMETHEUS

Thus the direction of the search for innocence has also shifted a good deal. We still live under the shadow of the fear that the self-assertion of Prometheus against God is the primal and prime sin. But now the guilt lies in submission to these other forms of the cosmocentric; the search for innocence lies more clearly in the creation of an anthropocentric world. Surely the search for innocence is the search for the self and the refusal to let it be altogether dissolved by space, by stars, by objects, by the will, by absolute technology, by any *single* ambition of the human. One of our most central literary images has been the dissolving self.

It can require every manner of resource, all kinds of imagining and searching, to find and restore the human self in new circumstances. The new Prometheus will usually be hard to recognize as such, for neither the language nor the scene can be the same. Everything will be more ordinary. It is like a real and profound changing of the guard. The scene will no longer be a bare and desolate mountain in the Caucasus.

Let me take the case of Samuel Beckett. Faced with the extraordinary complexities of the latest form of cosmological problem, the modern artist as new Prometheus does indeed resort to extreme stripping processes. He ventures his own "descent into hell" in an attempt to find the new pinpoint of the self underneath the new forms of the cosmos. As one reads the version of the descent he finds in the novels and plays of Beckett, it is not at all clear that the first Prometheus, back in the original cosmic darkness, had the harder task. But the

Irish writer is unique in combining two important ventures. He not only takes up the task of Prometheus as he searches for man under the form of the new cosmology. The extraordinary thing is that he combines this search with a search into the venture as failure. Failure is one neglected part of our total human situation. Beckett declares that the task of art is failure, but not in the usual sense that art is a successful examination of the tragic. He proposes to imagine the ultimate failure and impotency of art but to do it in a sense far removed from the French symbolists, who quit poetry when they came to their point of failure. Beckett's work only begins at the point of failure, impotency, helplessness. This is what he sets to imagining: the failure of his own art. If this is what he is doing, as he says it is and as I think it is, then this Prometheus may very well be a new hero in inserting that share of the consciousness of nothingness into Prometheanism which will keep it sane. To imagine nothingness, to give it a body, as the imagination must give a body in every case; without giving it a body, which is the task in this case—there is a task for the imagination! This is important for our image of secularity. Not that it must be reduced by religiosity to nothing—for then I am back in the very secular image I am fighting against—but nothingness must get into the image as part of it. (There are some writers who say "but not in the American image," but that is absurd. It's absurd to exclude the sense of the tragic and the sense of nothingness from the American image of reality.)

Let us see what can happen at the changing of the guard.

Within Beckett's theatrical world, in Endgame, in Happy Days, in Waiting for Godot, in Krapp's Last Tape, in All That Fall, in An Act Without Words, there is a reduction of objects to an absolute minimum. The cosmos has almost vanished. The first two scenic words of Endgame are: "bare interior." There is an armchair for the dying hero Hamm. There are two ashbins which will be found to contain his parents. The opening stage direction of Happy Days is: "Expanse of scorched grass rising centre to low mound. Gentle slopes down to front and either side of stage. Back an abrupter fall to stage level. Maximum of simplicity and symmetry." The principal character is increasingly embedded in the mound as the play moves along. For Waiting for Godot the scene reads: "A country road. A tree. Evening." The direction for the opening of the second and final act is:

"Next day. Same time. Same place." A critical part of the action will be a discussion as to whether the tree has really changed, whether there has been any real change of scene. In *Krapp's Last Tape* there is a small table with a tape recorder on stage. The first line of *Act Without Words* reads: "Desert. Dazzling light."

Man alone is now on the stage. He can be looked at without distraction, usually under a bright white light. But it would be a mistake to think that now that things are gone man will emerge. The important part of the imagination's stripping process has only begun. It tries everywhere to find the human being, to build him, but it cannot. Either there is a vanishing process going on, as in *Happy Days*, or a dying process, as in *Endgame*, or a not-even-able-to-remember process in *Godot*, as the characters struggle to remember identity or even the beginning of a sentence they have started. They try every little trick to fill the void (after all, as the first line of *Godot* says: "Nothing to be done"), but they fail, and the writer fails. But failure is his project. Not merely to fail but to imagine it.

In Beckett's novels the search for man is even barer and deeper. The critics do not agree on the meaning, but they all agree that the stripping process in modern art cannot go any further than in Beckett. They call him the end of a road; I am not sure that they mean this as a compliment or that they really believe Beckett when he says that the business of the artist is failure. The characters cannot get hold of anything with the mind, though the trying is endless. Or they begin to fall apart, to decompose, to crawl finally with face into the mud. Is some such descent always necessary to rediscover the human in the middle of every cosmological crisis? Is it possible that the question being asked is: Is it still human? If it is, it is the most compassionate of questions and answers. It is the question to be asked over against every cosmological image of the secular project. But beyond the form of the question in Beckett, if this is his question, how unconditional can you get about human unconditionality? For surely, in the secular project and image, there are no conditions that can be attached to the question: Is this a man? Are Africa and Asia human?

Beckett fails, man fails, but the man that fails is put back into the picture as man. This thing that fails is a man.

One last word about Beckett, in order to put two things together. I agree with Tindall that in the Irish writer there is an obsessive attention to particulars but that he might be telling us "I like to record things that seem to signify nothing in particular," and that with the help of Beckett we might reform our symbolist habits a little bit. "For whatever we say, his bicycle remains a bicycle and his pot a pot."[21] They need no meaning and are unconditional. But this is also true of a man, whether under stars or objects or mud. A man is unconditionally a man. In America or anywhere else any image of the secular, any act of the imagination short of this, leaves us guilty still, and still short on the road to innocence. For my own first and last word in this book will be that innocence and guilt reside in no secret place but in our images. We are guilty if we limit the image of man (or the image of the secular project) to a few corners of man, to a color, a class, or only to that which works.

The great revolution will be to leave nothing and nobody out of the image of the human. What could take more imagining than this? Perhaps one other thing. To leave nothing human out of the image of man. That is the best way to handle Prometheanism.

Some Final Points

So much for one instance of the search for man at a cosmocentric moment. I should like to say a few more things about our anthropocentric image of the secular project.

1. If we begin to see the great positive relations between the secular and the human adventures, we will begin to take a fearless view of the anthropocentric. The world can become so vast and frightening, and man so small and so anxious a pinpoint—gazing into space from his frightening edge of the mountain—that he always has to find or make a place where he is the center. This "human project" has only in passing been an attack on religion. (It only seemed to be "Promethean.") Nor need our own project share in the feelings or intentions of the older humanism of Babbitt and More of the 1920's, which was so cosmocentric and which insisted that the more cosmic and divine awe we have the more human we are. Surely if this was our problem then, it is not our problem now. For we had not only come to a point of awe. We had actually come to a point of fright and a deep point of anxiety before the discoveries of an incredible universe by the secu

lar exploration. And we had been driven by it into a small and Manichean image of ourselves. The anthropocentric reaction was not only valid and true; it was also a matter of life and death.

2. The reversed image means that all things in the universe are in some way or other to be translated into the forms of man so far as their meaning goes. They will all take on the shapes, forms, colors, the frames of reference of his mind and his senses. (There is no such thing as a pure object untouched by the spirit of man or not reduced to one of his forms or images). This will in no way imply a deformation of objects, as though there were first an object in a pure state that is then distorted by the mind or imagination of man. Nor does such an anthropological proposition interfere with any real objectivity of such a hypothetical object. To make a thing or situation more human does not make it at all less objective, and as a matter of fact, a "pure poetry" or a "pure architecture" is a delusion. They ought also to be purely human. The unconditionality with which our image started must become the unconditionality of the forms of man. But that does not mean there was a previous unconditionality of a purer state.

3. For what I hypothesize is that objects in their structure and reality are in a very deep relation and correspondence with the mind, senses, and heart of man. Let us imagine that there has been a double incarnation, one at the creation and the other at the birth of Christ. We put on the mind of God in faith, but let us suppose that twice God put on our mind with which to think. The first time He did it He made the world. He made it according to all the things that have parallelism and resonance for the body and the spirit of man: its density to touch, its light and its colors to see, its sounds to hear; it is only when the two come together, man and the world, that the world becomes what it is. It might simplify the whole discussion of unconditionality versus metaphysics if we remember, therefore, that the world was made not according to "divine" but human ideas.

4. The odyssey and the project of man is a march through man himself. The most important kind of time for man is the kind that exists within himself, existing in the form of the stages of his own life: birth, childhood, adolescence, prime, middle age, old age, and death. He is moving thus through himself in order to get somewhere. The time structure of man is a movement that is meant to get somewhere. Only permanent children get stuck and get nowhere. But there are a

thousand counterimages of secularity which get bogged down in the mire of some single point; they are afraid of the passage through the human; they heroize youth; they are especially afraid of death.

5. Next I would like to speak of the relation of Christ to this anthropological image. In another place I have suggested this picture of the relationship.

The phases of the life of man are the mysteries of man. . . .

The phases of the life of Christ are the mysteries of Christ. But it is the time and the phases, the odyssey of man, which he re-explored. . . .

The Son of God is the Sun, but the course of this Sun is · through man. Above all, he is, in this coursing, a bridegroom (*et ipse tamquam sponsus, procedens a thalamo suo*) and an athlete (*exultavit ut gigas ad currendam viam suam*) running with joy (*desiderio desideravi*) through the whole length and breadth of the human adventure (*a summa coelo egressio ejus usque ad summum ejus*). He marches to the ultimate of the human (*usque ad mortem*). Wherefore he has been exalted and every knee shall bow to him, of all the things that are in heaven or on earth or under the earth . . . . it is the perfect sign and accomplishment of the mysteries or stages of human life, that they are, on a level much more intense than ever before, an intrinsic path to God. We miss the point if we only say that Christ is the gate and do not also add that man is the gate. It is our recurring mystery of more than one level in the one act and in the one fact.[22]

6. Our human image of the secular project can now take a final anthropocentric step. It can propose that the direction and movement of the project be based on the wishes of man. Man is the forger of his own destiny. The only thing asked of him is that he remain a man.

ACT TWO

The Search for Light

I

The Old Hypothesis

The secular project must now become an image of that which is free and open, inhibited by nothing save that which is human. This freedom and openness takes the shape of a constant dramatic passage from old to new hypothesis, from old to new image. But the passage is not achieved without suffering. In what follows we imagine the three phases of any secular movement into new light: the old hypothesis, the passage, the new hypothesis. They bring us further and further away from all those mechanical and lifeless images of secularity within which neither the religious nor the secular imagination could live and breathe.

Thus far we imagine secularity not as a journey through the cosmos but as a journey through man, not as a submission by man to the endless unconditionality of the cosmological but as the passage of every independent system through the unconditionality of the human, not as a Promethean but a human project. But if we go no further we would be tempted to imagine a great free project as always submitting to a fixed human point; we would be imagining the human as fixed, as limit, as boundary, as law, as guardian and forger of fear for forgers of projects. Therefore we come now to the image of the human (and the human project) as open and free.

If the human has the authority to fasten its unconditionality upon every species of the cosmological and on every form of endlessness, that does not mean it is not itself open. The human is open in itself and open in the "space" always left to it for its freedom; the human project is identical with the life of the imagination itself. For it is a perpetual passage from old to new hypothesis. In the present chapter I propose to ask what this passage means. I shall continue to take the help of Aeschylus in asking and answering the question.

75

Freedom within the project is also our chapter question. But freedom is a vacuous thing without a body and I wish to give it such a body as belongs to the central issues of this book. I wish to equate the state of freedom with the state of our images. A man does not move into freedom without a transformation of images. I shall turn again to Aeschylus for an example of such a transforming movement into freedom.

There is no freedom without the transformation of our images. Freedom is not a thing we add to a man; it is a state of everything in man, but especially a state of his images. We can perform a thousand heroic feats of the will; this will be only a substitute and an imitation of that substantive freedom which can only come by changing our images from old to new. For example, the whole of modern psycho-analytical theory is based on the ideal of a freedom that comes from the transformation of images. I have noted how it confronts the tyranny of certain past events as they shape and trap our images of the present; it proposes to introduce us to the freedom of the reality in front of us by exposing the ubiquitous presence of dead images and hypotheses; its essential task is to change the images from rigidity to freedom, to set them in motion. This itself means a movement from old to new hypotheses. Again we are back in the image of the trap and the movement out of it.

First a short interlude on the relation between *hypothesis* and *image*.

As I now begin to use the two words *image* and *hypothesis*, they mean the same thing. Therefore the struggle for a new hypothesis is a struggle for a new image and vice versa. In both cases we are struggling for a new way of looking at things. At present I am struggling for a new religious image of secularity.

Any fact is contained within a way of looking at things, within a context, within a pattern, within an image, within a hypothesis, within a vocabulary. There is, I repeat, no such thing as a pure fact that is not contained within a hypothesis or image or way of looking at things. A new hypothesis (and an image) is a new colligating or binding together of "facts" by a new conception (or image). But we must not suppose that the image or hypothesis is a later addition to a fact or set of facts. The "facts" must be seen in some way or other and the some-way-or-other is the hypothesis or image.

The world is coming at us all day long, and we at it; we handle it with amazing successions of hypotheses or images. I step into a room and elect those spatial lines in it which make it a habitation and a home. I go out of the room and as I do I rearrange everything into a new image of a place which leads into an outer and a greater world. All the day long I form and re-form the world, moving from image to image, trying never to submit to endlessness or senselessness. All human thought has this quality of conquering chaos; it is a constant conquest of the purely cosmological. A good deal of mental illness can be understood if it is seen as an inability, much below the normal threshold, to cope with oncoming reality by the ordinary procedures of new image and new hypothesis. The imagination is trapped.[1]

But mental illness is only an extreme example; a whole culture may fail, over a very long period, to break out of a dead into a new hypothesis. This is largely what Aeschylus was talking about in the whole of the *Oresteia*. This was the thematic note of my prologue. Let me therefore look at some of the "facts" of this prototype as the human race struggles within an old hypothesis for a new vision. It is trying to break out of a trap, as we are in our day.

On the surface Aeschylus is dealing with the dramatic history of a long sequence of terrible facts that began way back in the history of the house of Atreus. This is the simplest thing that is happening, before the plot thickens and the image with it.

There is the crime of Thyestes against the wife of his brother Atreus.

There is the avenging crime of Atreus against Thyestes as he serves the latter with his own children to eat.

Thereafter each side of the family is striking back at the other as the generations move on. With Aeschylus we begin to call the whole chain the chain of the Furies. There is a Fury sitting upon this house; but we shall see that this Fury is not only a god but an active hypothesis about the nature of reality. The hypothesis is tribal and equalizing vengeance.

And the Furies shall now split husband and wife, Agamemnon and Clytemnestra, according to the more ancient split.

Agamemnon sacrifices his daughter Iphigeneia in order to appease the gods and win safety for his fleet against Troy.

Aegisthus (of the progeny of Thyestes) seduces Clytemnestra, wife of Agamemnon (of the lineage of Atreus).

On his return from Troy as victor Agamemnon is slain by Clytemnestra in vengeance for Iphigeneia.

The son Orestes emerges as avenger and slays his mother and Aegisthus. He uses the same weapon as had slain his father.

Now, as the second play ends and the third play begins, the Furies pursue Orestes in a new act of vengeance.

After enormous suffering and a great public trial, after a great confrontation between the wisdom of Athena and the justice of the Furies, Orestes is released, the courts of human civilization begin, Athens is founded as city of man, and the gods (the Furies and Athena) are reconciled. We shall see that what has happened is the progressive and dramatic emergence of a new hypothesis about the human reality.

I say that these are the *surface* facts. They are in reality not pure facts at all but only have existence within an image or hypothesis. The "facts" are always contained within the old or the new hypothesis. The old hypothesis had been seen as an image of reality itself. This hypothesis or image may be thus put: Human action and interaction must form a perfect, mathematical equation. Whatever you do must with precision be done unto you. The hypothesis is vengeance; the hypothesis is mathematical justice. The Furies behind the cosmos are not satisfied until action has produced perfect reaction and everything is thus reckoned, counted, and put back in place. In each case it is this hypothesis, this image of human reality, that causes the next step. I would not have been able to list the facts without the hypothesis. It is fixed, absolute, and closed. Thus far it seems impossible to break out of it. It is precise, mathematical, implacable, perfectly rational. Its logic is unassailable. Here, at this moment in Greece, the chorus declares the law (and the hypothesis) to Orestes: "It is but law that when the red drops have been spilled upon the ground they cry aloud for fresh blood" (*The Libation Bearers*, ll. 400–404). Orestes decides, according to the vision of the old hypothesis, that if his mother has slain his father then he must slay his mother. And he decides on the need of a further equation. Even the same net shall be used against Clytemnestra that helped slay Agamemnon in the bath: "As they by treachery killed a man of high degree, by treachery, entangled in the self-same net they too shall die" (ll. 556–558). Thus the exact balance is restored and nature is put right. This is the supposition.

It is necessary to realize that in its own times this hypothesis can often have been a noble achievement.

For example, the other side of the gamut of ideas run through by the long and varied history of the word *Furies* is that of Justice, and this is the noblest, the most cosmic part of its history. The Furies are Dike; Dike, so conceived, is a Justice that will strike back at anything that moves out of its proper, ordained, and natural place in the universe. It will literally strike this thing back into its place. After the *Oresteia* there is hardly a more notable use of the image of the Furies among the Greeks than the tremendous place in the cosmic scheme of things assigned to them by Heraclitus: "The sun could not go out of his course without the Erinyes, ministers of justice, finding him out."[2]

Everything in its place. How nobly this concept of justice was used by Plato, at the very heart of the structure of *The Republic*, to explain the nature of the good within the human soul. But we must return to Prometheus himself if we are to understand some of the fantasies that have been generated by what we might call this spatial image of justice, of things in their place, of the terror when they are not. In the *Prometheus* Dike, Justice, is a creation of Zeus; it establishes the place of man over against the place of the gods; it is like a ditch between them. And one cannot help but think that the religious imagination has set itself up at times as a Fury, to question the drive of secularity toward autonomy, and to drive it back, often in an inhibiting way, across this ditch, into and under a world of religious symbols. It is still tempted toward the same refrain: "Only Zeus is free." But secularity itself does not need religion to create terror for it as it moves further and further into the far country on the other side of the ditch. The crossing generates its own terrors. And the most important Furies of all are secular, at the heart of the secular order.

Perhaps the most fascinating, the most revealing, of all the images of the Furies was their genealogy and place in early Greek cosmology, together with all the implications this genealogy has for our story. Here it is better to be general than to be too specific and so heavily burdened with genealogies that we might miss the forest for the trees. The world and the time the Furies belong to is the earliest, the most primitive (but indeed magnificent) period of Greek religion, where we can say that it is earth and nature, and the most elemental forces of both, that are directing the imagination in its mythologizing. It is our mighty Earth itself that is the primal goddess, begetting all other things and receiving them back again into herself. She begets or represents the deepest forces of nature and the most elemental human facts: procreation, blood, birth, the heavens, the ocean, marriage, fertility. The most fundamental facts, forms, and needs of nature are the first sanctities. The divine emerges as an earthy and dark force which places enormous emphasis on the eternal needs, shapes, and ordinances of nature. Within this system the Furies, daughters of the Night, are the awesome defenders and avengers of these profound and basic elements of earth, birth, and the whole world of "the natural."

I think we would be on the right track if we supposed that this whole earlier mythology, cosmology, and chthonic religion of the Greeks was an ancient hypothesis that was on the march toward the new Olympian religion. And we should accept this idea of development within the theology of Aeschylus himself.[3] The transformation of the image of the Furies is thus caught within this larger perspective of transformation. Within the thought and imagining of Aeschylus there is transformation in Zeus himself. But the transformation of the Furies, as it is recorded by Aeschylus in *The Eumenides*, is surely one of the most important steps in the movement of human civilization. The artist, however, is more than a recorder. In this case the monumental imagination of Aeschylus in the *Oresteia* is also still helping to create and reenforce the new visions. For the mastering of a more human vision of justice and the natural was not reached overnight or in a single stroke. It involved a long, hard struggle. Let us turn our attention to this period of travail in human imagining.

II

The Passage

In Scene Two we are in full passage between old and new image or hypothesis. It is the most typically human and least mechanical phase in our image of the secular project. It is a moment of suffering that is absolutely essential to the image. Now Orestes is out of touch with the old hypothesis, because now he knows it does not work and is a hopeless trap; but he is not yet in touch with the new. This is where we are, at our moment of the secular project. It is the price to be paid in the search for light.

In every department of secular and human reality there is some intermediacy between old and new image that begins to declare the death of the old and the struggle for the new. Every field must give its own example of intermediate travail and growth. Part of the pain comes from a temporary inability to define the problem and the hypothesis connected with it in each case, to keep it separate from every other. Thus, for example, with the hypothesis of organization. This one word must be broken down into a number of hypotheses. The hypothesis within the form of political nationalism as organization is beginning to break down and to demand a wider human organization, for our very survival's sake. As a total political solution it has been bypassed by history. We need a world government of some kind. On the other hand the hypothesis of bureaucratic organization in economics is going through a completely different travail. Whatever the new hypothesis will be, we sense that the old structures are so wide that they are in many ways inimical to the truly human. Modernization is essential but would it not have been possible to keep the smaller human line within the larger line? The proliferation behind this bureaucratic hypothesis is endless and for the time being out of hand to the point of fright. We are in passage between

With the vast amount of change always going on maybe an ideal of change is best?

hypotheses. In every such case the old hypothesis slowly becomes dead and dank, is no longer working, and will enter into a period of suffering. But I repeat: It is essential to be able to name the problem and not to lump all needs for revolution under the blanket of one revolution. For this would itself be a bureaucratic act of the imagination, or no act of the imagination at all. This is part of what I mean by the phrase *revolution without imagination.*

It is these intermediate periods in the dramatic history of secularity that are difficult and dangerous. They are periods of hopelessness, because our very definitions of reality have collapsed and are no longer working. The repetition of that which is not working is very difficult to endure.

There is plenty of evidence that we are passing through a profoundly painful intermediate period, in a way and degree that is not satisfied by the shibboleths that modern man must become a man of change. Something particularly painful must be happening. There is hardly a single hypothesis of social organization that is not being questioned. There is also an inability to project new hypotheses or else an inability to act according to them. The sociologists define this state as anomie, or normlessness.

I have given my own hypothesis (in the Prologue) that part of our pain comes from the new shocks involved in the vast contemporary advances of the secular project—where the quantitative step forward is so vast that it represents a qualitatively new situation. I have proposed that as a result we are in a period of revulsion away from the present situation of the project. It is a good and a bad revulsion. The project itself (the hypothesis) does need perpetual criticism, and who can doubt that at this point in its history it is contaminated with every manner of dehumanizing element. But I repeat that there is a good deal of fear and guilt *about the hypothesis and the project itself.* It is almost as though it were also being questioned in its essence, as it has been in other stages of advance, and often by those who declare themselves the most liberal spirits among us. There is a fear of advance and a love of guilt in the air. There are fierce waves of evangelical and passionate guilt sweeping our own nation; the guilt is so intense and the search for even an approximate, a small taste of innocence so important, that I have devoted a separate section to the problem and will wait till then to talk at any length about it. In the meantime I simply propose that neither those who are possessed, hysterically, by absolute guilt or absolute innocence are going to make any contribution toward humanizing the human race or the project or anything else. This apparently opposing possession by guilt or innocence is another form of the apparently deep gap between the far Left and the far Right: Underneath all the conflict they are brothers; their attack on each other is also an embrace.

At any rate we are going through a period of self-questioning and of the questioning of some of our most fundamental hypotheses. It is also a dangerous period because the temptation, when no way out is yet seen, is to lash out at other groups and to substitute violence for the imagination. This is especially true when the magnificent ideal of secularity itself (universal identity, emergence, and salvation) is not seen as dramatic and historical but only as pure idea. For where the failures and sufferings of the ideal meet with no historical image or dramatic idea they will be all the more intolerable. We saw that this collapse of the dramatic and historical sense will lead to every form of moral absolutism and idealism, and may God help those who get in its way. This refusal to accept any gap between ideal and reality is, ironically, one of the worst forms of Prometheanism.

These intermediate moments, then, are dangerous, but it would be even more dangerous not to recognize the symptoms of such moments of history, not to recognize what has become dead or hopeless, not to choose to imagine our way out of it. Usually we cannot predict the moment of the emergence of the new hypothesis or image, but I think that we can often declare the occurrence of this prelude, this intermediate period, this time of failure, hopelessness, inoperancy. We are in this period in relation to the forms of social organization. I think that this is the mid-period we are in with relation to the religious image of secularity. We sense that to remain within our previous and older images of secularity may prove disastrous.

Let me try to summarize the signs in Orestes as he passes through the intermediate time. How does he know that the time of passage has come? Though he does not see the way out, he begins to see:

1. that the old hypothesis is a fixed and rigid trap;
2. and that it does not work.

The old hypothesis is seen as fixed, absolute, and rigid, a trap. That was my opening metaphor. It is customary to say that conflict is the heart of the dramatic process, but this statement often does as much to hide the real dramatic process as reveal it. Here, for example, in this history lived long ago at Mycenae, it is only on the surface that there is conflict; the truly dramatic point is that there is none. On the surface there is the conflict of Orestes: I should, I should not, slay my mother. But the major task of the trilogy is to create the image of an old hypothesis within which there is neither real conflict, nor choice, nor alternative. Let me develop this statement.

With Orestes the imagination, whether it acts or does not act (whether he slays his mother or not) is caught in the old mathematical image of vengeance, the image of the permanent, exact balance of the universe. The choice of action or non-action, of the slaying or not slaying of his mother, is really of no consequence, although it is dramatically important to reveal that it is of no consequence. For either course will occur within the system of vengeance and equalization, and neither course will bring an end to the endless chain. Yes or no will produce vengeance. He actually chooses to slay his mother. And the Furies, as curse of his mother, descend avengingly upon the avenger, "the bloodhounds of my mother's hate." But let us hypothesize that he chose not to act. Even then, I say, let us not be deceived. The hypothesis, the act of the imagination, would have been really the same. The terms and limitations of the vision are the same: punishment, vengeance, equalization—now from the curse of a father unavenged.

It may be worthwhile to quote at length this scene from *The Libation Bearers* to describe the terror of Orestes before this other and identical and now paternal half of the same hypothesis from which the imagination cannot yet escape:

Orestes
　　The big strength of Apollo's oracle will not
　　forsake me. For he charged me to win through this hazard,
　　with divination of much, and speech articulate,
　　the winters of disaster under the warm heart
　　were I to fail against my father's murderers;
　　told me to cut them down in their own fashion, turn

to the bull's fury in the loss of my estates.
He said that else I must myself pay penalty
with my own life, and suffer much sad punishment;
spoke of the angers that come out of the ground from those
beneath who turn against men; spoke of sicknesses,
ulcers that ride upon the flesh, and cling, and with
wild teeth eat away the natural tissue, how on this
disease shall grow in turn a leprous fur. He spoke
of other ways again by which the avengers might
attack, brought to fulfillment from my father's blood.
For the dark arrow of the dead men underground
from those within my blood who fell and turn to call
upon me; madness and empty terror in the night
on one who sees clear and whose eyes move in the dark,
must tear him loose and shake him until, with all his bulk
degraded by the bronze-loaded lash, he lose his city.
An such as he can have no share in the communal bowl
allowed them, no cup filled for friends to drink. The wrath
of the father comes unseen on them to drive them back
from altars. None can take them in nor shelter them.
Dishonored and unloved by all the man must die
at last, shrunken and wasted away in painful death.[4]

What is happening is that the imagination of Orestes, whether it acts maternally or paternally, is trapped.

The advance made—through the period of passage and endlessness—is that the imagination no longer sees the old hypothesis as definition of reality and truth but sees, in suffering, that it is stuck, trapped. It is trapped in its own net. For the time being there is no way out. In Orestes the house of Atreus comes to this new point of passage. The imagination is still thrashing about against the walls of the old hypothesis, but the description of the situation begins to be entirely different. It is only now that true conflict can begin to appear.

For every previous statement about the old hypothesis was a statement that it works, that it is a resolution and a way out. Everyone is caught but at least hopes that the hypothesis will be a successful resolution. The supposition behind every action taken (from the feast for Thyestes to the Trojan War, to the slaying of Agamemnon,

Aegisthus, and Clytemnestra) is based on the supposition that the action, because it is identical action, will set things right. But in no case does it actually work. It always leaves guilt; it never reaches innocence; it always leaves a shadow; it always requires a new vengeance; it is always endless, but not yet seen to be so. One would expect that at least in the case of Cassandra, with all her capacity for understanding of the past and prophecy for the future, there would be a breakthrough. Yet even her furthest reach of imagining, as in vision she watches the murder of Agamemnon, is to declare that Orestes will come as avenger. It is Orestes who cries out, at the close of *The Libation Bearers:* Where is there an ending?

Now it is at last clear that Orestes has brought nothing to an end. The trilogy has reached the point where it cannot go on with the same story, though it is its own achievement that it brings us to this point.

This, then, is an analogue for all such intermediate moments of the imagination. Apparently it is a necessary intermediacy before transformation. It is a recurrent point in the secular project. It is the time of suffering ($\pi\alpha\theta\circ\varsigma$). It is also a period which is tempted to solve everything by violent thrusts of the will and not by imagination.

This is the way in which the dramatic imagination works through passage in Aeschylus. But it is not too far from the way in which the scientific or the philosophical mind works at its best. None of these processes starts with clarity, but each tries to end with it. The latest definition of the work of contemporary philosophy could have been taken from an analysis of the *Oresteia*, written in the year 458 B.C. A critic refers to an article by John Wisdom as "a landmark in the history of philosophy" and continues:

> The first significant thing about the article is its title, "Philosophical Perplexity". It had always been assumed that the job of philosophers was to answer questions, to solve problems. . . . What philosophers said would be true or false, even if only in the sense in which tautologies are true and contradictions false. But this title suggests that philosophers are not propounding solutions to problems, answering questions, putting forward theories, but are rather grappling with puzzlement, trying to put themselves straight where they are confused; to do philosophy is less like trying to discover

some elusive facts than trying to find one's way out of a maze. A favourite way of putting this point was to say that philosophical problems needed not to be solved but to be dissolved. All this cannot, of course, be grasped from the title alone, but it is reasonable to suppose that such considerations were in the author's mind when he chose the title.[5]

In every case what is required is a description, in some detail, of the way in which the mind or imagination is stuck, is puzzled, is caught, and knows it—which is an altogether different moment from the moment of rigidity. Had there been more space, I would have liked to examine in further detail the forward movement of awareness within the imagination of Aeschylus in the Oresteia. He is a master at imagining the endlessness that comes before vision. For example, a close examination of the extraordinary metric of the trilogy will reveal that the powerful and repetitive use of certain specific meters, especially the dochmiac, is contributing enormously, through ninetenths of the three plays, to the creation of the image of aggressive and repetitive endlessness. There is also the cumulative power of a vast number of sub-images under two main images in the trilogy:

1. The image of the trap or net;
2. The image of light and dark, as human beings succeed in acting only to find tragic residues of that which has not worked. What is involved is an analysis of the total act by which Aeschylus imagines endlessness. Artists are called upon to imagine strange and difficult things. There was Beckett imagining failure and nothing. Here is Aeschylus imagining endlessness, our awareness of endlessness in the old hypothesis before we transform it into new.

It is not an abstract problem, this legacy of endlessness in the imagination, but one with which many of our own artists struggle. It is a preoccupying modern problem; I would like to name some of its names and forms; however different they all are, they all agree that we have on our hands a radical and tormenting disease of the imagination, an endlessness which might mean that something in us cannot endure the unconditionality we discovered in the imagination.

There are good imaginers around us and they have imagined endlessness well with their pictures of the endless, repetitive act: Jean-Paul Sartre in No Exit; Brecht in Baal; Ionesco in The Lesson; Beckett in nearly everything he has written; Kafka in *The Trial* and *The Castle*; Camus in *Sisyphus*; Sartre again in the whole strucure of his metaphysics of *Being and Nothing*, where man is a cat never catching up with his tail; and how many plays are there where the thing that has happened is about to happen again? We are beset with the image and the state of endlessness.

I am concerned with the fundamental endlessness of a secularity cut off from the broad totality of human sensibility. This counter-image comes out more clearly when we turn to the world of objects. Something that preoccupies many a modern artist is any endless *proliferation* of objects that has its own separate life and unconditionality, an independent world with no relation to the human. Sheer proliferation is a frequent image. In Ionesco, it is chairs, chairs, chairs, chairs, chairs, in a riotous image of the point. In Sartre it is this endless proliferation of things, like a jungle that in its growth will finally conquer the city of man, that is part of the cause of the nausea at things. But in a sociologist like Thorstein Veblen you get the same image, in more analytic and evidential forms.

Here the image I want myself to recall is my own image of the cosmological. To the degree that this unconditional nonhuman proliferation of objects develops, you get the return of another form of the cosmological situation for man. But instead of being a pinpoint lost in awful space among the endless stars, he feels himself thus situated in a new world of objects and sensation. He has not yet forced the new world into his terms. He has not yet built an inside that can handle the great new world. There are too many things, too many people, too many sensations, too many alternatives for action. It seems impossible to stop the proliferation, the escalation, the endlessness. The stars were a minor cosmological problem and never bothered men as much as we say they did, and there was this obvious advantage about the stars that they provided space to breathe. But now there is no space left; it has been taken away by objects; nobody knows how to turn the process off; there is the beginning of an altogether new kind of cosmological insecurity in the air; there is a subterranean panic that does not yet call itself by that name because it hides itself under the form of violence, as insecurity always does. It is the return of the *cosmological* image of secularity that is doing it.

That image has always bred panic, insecurity, and violence. But it is not the number of objects that matters; we have not yet developed a confident interior life to help us live and breathe in this world.

III

The New Hypothesis

The image of secularity is always climbing or reaching to some such stage of a new hypothesis as now lies before us. Orestes fights clear of the trap and the puzzlement. The new hypothesis is a moment of equity, wisdom, humanity, the bringing of endlessness to an end. It knows that a new moment has come that is full of meaning. This is the way Athens or the city of man was founded. Now perhaps we must move toward a still newer hypothesis and a larger city of man. It is a large example of the movement within secularity.

We have examined the hypothesis that had been passed on to Aeschylus and that he had put into question. It is the hypothesis of the Furies, of violent and equal reaction, of mathematical justice, of implacable logic in human affairs, of endlessness. As we resume with the new hypothesis, it will be to ask how man might transform these images. The question will be: how to see the "facts" (here it is the facts of the house of Atreus) in a new light. It is not true that we are in a passionate search for new facts. We are after new light for the same facts.

A new hypothesis is a new pattern or a rearrangement of facts—a new arrangement or understanding within which the facts can remain the same or are a combination of old and new facts. In very many cases it is a new set of facts that demand the new image. But it may be identical materials that are incorporated into the new understanding.

Ideally the old hypothesis is incorporated into the new, so that there is a real transformation and not a destruction of the old. Ideally the new hypothesis does not skip the historical and transforming process which is involved in the formation of the new. It does not opt for magical and absolutized acts of the imagination which have no history and therefore cannot possibly have a future. There are factors that account for the fascination of absolute ideas that have no history. They do not need explanation and are neither accountable nor responsible. They give the feeling of salvation. They create the ground for an elite group that can alone understand the new hypothesis. This is an enviable position to be in.

The new Left fits into this pattern and position in more ways than one. One of its central qualities is that it is a corruption of a long honored type of thought and action in western civilization which we call dialectical and which, in my present context, demands that every *is*, every fact, every status quo, stand perpetually in the critical presence of its renewing or reforming or transforming Idea or real ideal. This demands a constant back and forth between *is* and *ought*. The deepest corruption of this idea occurs when the relationship becomes one between absolute good and absolute bad. The function of the Idea is to destroy the fact. The *Idea* of the new Left feels no responsibility to explain itself (or to imagine itself) in terms of new or intermediate facts. It is therefore to its advantage, indeed it is altogether necessary to its strategy, that it cancel out free speech and refuse to answer questions. For the very nature of dialectical thought is a constant question and answer relationship in which *ought* is always questioning *is* and *is* is always questioning *ought*. The thought finally occurs that under the weight of such a corruption of the dialectical and under the weight of such a refusal to imagine the beginnings of a new future, the new Left must surely be seized with the occasional uneasy fear that its absolute ideas are not really revolutionary.

It is ironic that Athena, the central character in the final hypothesis of Aeschylus, has also become the symbol of an action of the imagination which is the very opposite of that transforming process through which she is about to lead us. A legend tells us that she was born, full grown, from the head of Zeus, without growth, without a past relationship, a true absolute that only imitates the constantly new unconditionality of history which with her help we are about to study.

For over against the whole past of the house of Atreus, Athena does indeed introduce a totally new vision; but it will be a transforming vision.

After long and purifying travail, after a long period of agonizing pursuit by the Furies of his mother, Orestes follows the dictate of Athena: He comes to Athens to stand trial before the newly created court of the Areopagus, a group that can represent all human courts and all reachings for truly human decisions on the part of the emerging thing we can call the city of man. When a whirlwind of rational argument for and against Orestes in that trial gets nowhere and ends in an equal vote for and against him, Athena herself casts a deciding vote on the side of an ending; she declares him released. But nowhere does the goddess declare that he has not committed a crime; nowhere does she exonerate him. Nor does she anywhere reject or dishonor the Furies; in the very action of freeing Orestes she declares that the new city of man, which is now transforming the savage mathematical ways of the feudal families and tribes, shall never be able to do without the reality and terror of justice. She welcomes the Furies into the city; she does not repress them or naïvely deny their existence.

We are at last in the presence of a new justice, but a justice nevertheless; not a justice destroyed but a justice transformed and humanized. The new hypothesis includes the old. What here intervenes, in the form of Athena, is the unconditional decision of the goddess which we can equate with equity. It is an example of that simple victory over the indeterminate which is the simplest and the best mark of the human and which will not tolerate the inhumanity of the endless. It is not a rejection of justice but a governing of it and a refusal to give it its head; to give it complete freedom means madness. It is an endless trap.

Athena, though a goddess, represents that constant intervention of the human over endlessness which is its own authority, but which is only authoritative as often as it emerges as human solution.

Athena was facing the violent demands of many contrary forces that had been tearing the beginnings of civilization to pieces by their unyielding quarrels. By her intervention she must have reminded of those great figures who had arisen in the past to exercise decisive imagination over the boundless hatreds of the political order. Of all these Solon had been the greatest. As mediator and almost as redeemer he had used an extraordinary combination of force and justice to rebuff every form of madness. And he could proudly say: "Between the two armies I held firm." So that a great historian like Glotz could rightly say in summary: "It is in this spirit of heroic impartiality, with the firm intention of writing equal laws for great and small, that Solon set about liquidating the past and preparing the future."[6]

It was in the same spirit that Aeschylus, as poet and teacher, had taken up his own task of reconciliation between the cosmological and the human forces in the history of man. Through the embodying spirit of Athena and Athens he brings the chthonic and the Olympian forces of Greek religion together; he introduces humanity into the midst of the terror images of the world and of justice; he reconciles the Furies and Zeus. Like a new Solon, a Solon of the imagination, he stands between opposing armies of images and brings them peace.

But he does not stoop to the romantic solution, nor does he minimize the terror, as the men of the Enlightenment still tend to do. The terror and the justice are not denied, they are taken hold of and still honored; they are not dissolved by some cute trick of the imagination; the Furies are transformed but not evicted:

> There shall be peace forever between these people
> of Pallas and their guests. Zeus the all seeing
> met with Destiny to confirm it.
> Singing all follow our footsteps.[7]

These are the very last lines of the great trilogy, spoken by a procession within which all contending parties, getting below all faction and ideology, unite at the level of a new vision and a new hypothesis. If only we can do it again.

The action of Athena in *The Eumenides* has been an act which terminates the purely mathematical history of the house of Atreus and brings it into the light of a totally new world. Like every new hypothesis this action is a totally new act of the imagination, a new pattern or rearrangement of old and new facts, a new creation. It is equity, it is wisdom, it is persuasion, it is humanity, it is the human gift, beyond all reason, of declaring an ending to endlessness.

It says: I have been standing *there* all my life; now let me change and stand *here*, so that I see from a new vantage. I have been standing on the earth; now let me stand on the sun; or now let me choose any point in the universe as its center; or let me look for some Archimedean point outside my whole system of things from which I can lift the world with new vision. In the case of the house of Atreus part of the new assumption, hitherto forbidden, is: Let us imagine that we do not strike back at Orestes. Or if we strike, let it be wisdom and not a feudal descendant that strikes back. Aeschylus is not interested in the passage out of feudalism for its own sake; it is also a metaphor for all such transitions of the imagination. Thus what is involved here is no mere intellectual hypothesis; there is also a proposal for a totally new hypothesis of feeling and passion. For the forces contending before Athena, Apollo, and the Furies are not only godly or demonic figures but represent powerful sets of human feelings that had been built into Greek civilization as ultimate assumptions behind human actions.

The vision of Athena, as mistress of the arts and the imagination, was entirely different. She represented the breakthrough of civilization into a larger human vision and the conquest of man over barbarism. It was no wonder, therefore, that the great sculptures of the Parthenon that had been erected in her honor could celebrate victory after victory of the human over the dark forces of the universe. There was the victory of the Lapiths over the only half human and savage centaurs. There was the victory over the Amazons, and the victory of the new race of Olympian gods over the Giants. At another point (a sad metaphor) there was the story of the defeat of Troy. Perhaps most beautiful of all, there was the subject of the extraordinary east pediment of the Parthenon, commemorating the precise moment of the birth of Athena herself, to which I have already referred. Even the incomplete Elgin marbles tell us with what precision and clarity this new moment must have been caught. It is a moment of transition, a victory of light over darkness. The aspiring head of the horse of the Sun still moves through the first moment of his appearance out of the sea in the East; the weary horse of the Moon is disappearing exhausted in the West. We know that in the center was Zeus, and Athena new born from his head at the first moment of the dawn. Round all four sides of the new temple ran the full-of-motion friezes of the Panathenaic procession in honor of the Maid: the horsemen preparing, the horses prancing, the horsemen in line and at gallop, the chariots, the elders, the musicians, the tray bearers, the beasts who are to be victims, the maidens, the marshals, the magistrates, finally the gods themselves and the robing of Athena in her new gown. So close was the association of Athens and Athena. And so much did the city admire the mythical wisdom of the Maid. It is hard to think of a more beautiful carving out by men of a moment of new light.

Some twenty years before the carving of these friezes Aeschylus had represented his own Panathenaic processional in the theater of Dionysius. This processional ending to the *Oresteia* was celebration of the decision of Athena and celebration of the foundation of the city of man. For the hypothesis behind the decision is that important; it marks the foundation of that way of looking at things which makes a new civilization possible. Thus the trilogy, far from being a private and absolute moment of a solipsistic imagination, has done two things that are completely contrary to any concept of art as private and absolute fact: It had previously swept into the full dimensions of human history, in the form of the long story of the house of Atreus, and now, at its close, it seems to merge into the public order of the Panathenaic procession as commemoration of the hypothesis which made possible the very founding of this city of Athena.

The new hypothesis of Athena and of that founding of the city of man which she represents has a number of important qualities. It is a movement forward from a former trap into an open world. It is another assertion of the victory of human unconditionality over the pain of an endless situation. It moves into a new stage or point of human development and insight which, like all similar human achievements, possesses infinitely more freedom than we are wont to realize. The freedom enters not only into the movement forward of the secular project but also into that very unconditionality of the new stage or hypothesis which I have spoken of from the beginning of this book. These stages can be interpreted as absolute preexisting points, locked in the mind of God or in the world of preexisting truth. But it seems better to me to see them as points or stages made, not without suffering, by man himself, with the sole proviso in them that they be human. If we follow this way of imagining our project, we are saved again from that purely cosmological way of imagining it which says that we must be perpetually in search of predetermined truth as a path. Thus too we are saved from all those moralistic and false questions which harrow the human spirit, such as: If we had only followed another way, if we had only followed the right way in history. The only thing that can predetermine the human is the human and human decisions. It is absurd to call this absurdity or sin. But it *is* the most difficult of all the historical forms of the relationship between God and man.

This presence of a deep, inward freedom at the very heart of all the stages or points of the secular project is a remarkable quality. I shall be saying in a moment that part of the disturbance that occurs within the religious imagination (and the secular!) when it has this further freedom proposed to it is that the freedom is imagined in a nonhistorical and nondramatic way. But first of all let us look briefly at a few modern equivalents of Athena as new and free hypothesis.

How, for example, did Gregor Mendel move toward the critical grasp of the statistical axioms of genetics? How did Albert Einstein come to the point of making the speed of light an axiom in his construction of relativity? These are model questions that are asked by the mathematician and philosopher of science J. Bronowski in a paper originally given to a great convocation of scientists at Southern Illinois University in 1965.[8]

Bronowski's first answer is a tribute not to the precise truthfinding power of the great mind that is involved in every such situation but to its remarkable flexibility and openness:

> An obvious answer is that the great mind, like the small, experiments with different alternatives, works out their consequences for some distance, and thereupon guesses (much like a chessplayer) that one move will generate richer possibilities than the rest. But this answer only shifts the question from one foot to another. It still remains to ask how the great mind comes to guess better than another, and to make leaps that turn out to lead further and deeper than yours or mine.

He does not pretend to have the answer to that further question, but of one thing he is certain, that this new step is not fixed within any logic but is free:

> We do not know . . . and there is no logical way in which we can know, or can formalize the pregnant decision [note the use of

the word *decision*]. The step by which a new axiom is added cannot itself be mechanized. It is a free play of the mind, an invention outside the logical processes. This is the central act of imagination in science and it is in all respects like any similar act in literature. In this respect, science and literature are alike: in both of them, the mind decides to enrich the system as it stands by an addition which is made by an unmechanical act of free choice.

Thus we are freer than we realize. Mendel himself would not have been aware of the terrifying area of freedom that might confront the biologist and geneticist of a day to come as he begins to gaze into the possibility of determining the very shape and future of humanity itself. But at the same time that we are swept into a new world of infinite possibility and alternative, we know that we are not yet equipped to handle this vast openness that has so suddenly confronted us. We are in a period of passage and suffering.

We feel overwhelmed and panicky. It is not so much that we know we can now destroy the world. That, terrible as it is, may not be our worst problem. For even if we decide to live, we shall be faced with so many of the new struggles for new hypotheses. Now we live in old hypotheses as we struggle with new worlds. In one direction we have hardly gone further than Athena and her foundation of a city state, so nationalistic is the world. Everybody knows we need a world order, but the hypothesis remains in the condition of a strange dream. We know that education must be revolutionized and we sense that this modern campus, separated from the surrounding reality and monopolizing to itself, against that reality, the whole idea of schooling, may be beginning to be a huge anachronism. There are thousands of situations in the world that can become apprenticing and schooling situations. It will only be a drop in the bucket of this problem if we assign two weeks before Election Day to give students the time to influence national elections. Again, we still live in a divided world where labor works with its hands and the intellectual lives a life of the mind, in a world not daring to face the consequences of the bitter cultural divisions that result from this old hypothesis. The laborer is cut off from his own mind, and the intellectual, worse still, is alienated not from the middle class but from his own hands. A new hypothesis begins to emerge which says that we can work with our hands and read Shakespeare too. Meantime we suffer intensely from this old aristocratic hypothesis of the division between the classes, the class of the hands and the class of the head, a division firmly established (and not moved beyond by us) in *The Republic* of Plato. But we must now hypothesize that this is not, except superficially, a division between town and gown, between middle class and intellectuals; it is a division rooted, tragically, at the very heart of the act of education. It is an old hypothesis that cannot work in a vast democratic society.

I have said that I would like to add another word about the profoundly historical and dramatic character of the secular project and all its new hypotheses. For we will be filled with disturbing thoughts as we discover our own great freedom and openness for the future unless we realize that we are historical beings.

If, as a matter of fact, there is disturbance over such unmeasurable freedom, it is again only because we are conceiving the human in an unhistorical and nondramatic way. We would be thinking of it as pure thought or pure will forging an open future in completely open and nonhuman space. Thus we would again have fallen into the pattern of the cosmological. But what is free and moving forward into the open is a completely historical being who has lived and died through the density of an endless number of lives and deaths and is the human being made by all this. He is already a human being and not an abstraction or a sheer point of thinking mind or flashing will. It is only this already profound knowledge of the human which will be able to judge the open future, to judge whether it be human or not. Only *historical* man can approach the future with an act of the imagination rather than with a pure idea or an act of the will or a mighty passion. It is only when freedom is accompanied by the imagination that it will not be taken hold of, spuriously, by Prometheanism in any form. If freedom is not taken over by the imagination, if openness is not filled with imagining, then it will be filled by the inevitable limitations, by prophets, by evangelists, by fire, by the will, by power. I was going to say that there are no substitutes for the imagination. But unfortunately there are. There are the fakers, without imagination.

It still remains that the imagination is free. All that is asked of it is that it remain the imagination.

Thus in this chapter I conclude another "moment" in this

attempt at a new religious image of the secular order. That image began by imagining unconditionality, autonomy, and identity as the first high and permanent quality of the secular project. A further moment or element of the image was reached by compelling this unconditional project, without losing any of its own inwardness, to become first a human and then a fully human project (Act One). In this present chapter the element we have been adding to the picture is that the humanity of the project is not a closing point or a negative limit but is itself remarkably open and free. This is a new and vast moment, but neither does it cancel out anything that has gone before it. For all that is asked of this freedom and openness is that it remain human.

I have called this moment a search for light. Now we move into a search for innocence. For so many of our old images of secularity are flooded with guilt. Is it possible so to purify these images that we can become far better managers of the great burden of this guilt?

ACT THREE

The Search for Innocence

I

The Element of Terror

Far from being a mechanical and meaningless order, the image of the secular project now becomes full of good and evil and of almost incalculable human forces (principalities and powers) that struggle for an approach to innocence. Once again secularity is not a pure idea, nor is its innocence. The latter is only reached by a dramatic march through painful fantasy, through a history of violent aggression, and through every kind of tawdry imitation of itself. Is it not clear that it will take all the resources of the religious imagination to cope with such a reality and to help secularity toward innocence?

The fundamental Aeschylean rhythm of action and suffering, of back and forth, forward movement and check, thrust and guilt, reality and illusion, is almost a truism to historians and analysts of the secular project of mankind. The project is always in search of innocence.

I read a serious analytic history of the idea of modernization such as C. E. Black's *The Dynamics of Modernization* and I see immediately that the very rhythm of the book is a case in point. Black begins with a periodization of human history that is very much like the divisions of my own image of the secular project. He suggests, for simplicity's sake (but also for the truth of it), that there have been three great revolutionary transformations or moments in the human story. The first "was the emergence of human beings, about a million years ago. . . . This infinitely slow process may be termed a revolution by virtue of the significance of the differences that separate prehuman from human life, and when one examines the differences, the term does not seem extravagant."[1] This is the moment where I say Prometheus descended with fire to give the very first elements of human resource to our race.

I found them witless and gave them the use of their wits and made them masters of their minds.[2]

The second great revolution was the emergence of man (principally in three locations, the valley of the Tigris and Euphrates, the valley of the Nile, and the valley of the Indus) into the forms of civilized society and into the fuller realities. This was our own second image as we watched Aeschylus commemorate the founding of the human city in that subsequent but ancient home of the house of Atreus. Surely he was also memorializing the birth of Athens itself as glorious crown of this revolution.

The third supremely important moment for Black is our present moment (just as it is in the case of our discussion of the new problems raised for the religious imagination today).

The process of change in the modern era is of the same order of magnitude as that from prehuman to human life and from primitive to civilized societies; it is the most dynamic of the great revolutionary transformations in the conduct of human affairs. What is distinctive about the modern era is the phenomenal growth of knowledge since the scientific revolution and the unprecedented effort at adaptation to this knowledge that has come to be demanded of the whole of mankind. Man perceives opportunities and dangers that for the first time in human existence are global in character, and the need to comprehend the opportunities and master the dangers is the greatest challenge that he has faced.[3]

And the enormous thing called "modernization" is defined in the following way:

"Modernization" as it is used here refers to the dynamic form that the age-old process of innovation has assumed as a result of the explosive proliferation of knowledge in recent centuries. It owes its special significance both to its dynamic character and to the universality of its impact on human affairs. It stems initially from an attitude, a belief that society can and should be transformed, that change is desirable. If a definition is necessary, "modernization" may be defined as the process by which historically evolved institutions are adapted to the rapidly changing functions that reflect the unprecedented increase in man's knowledge, permitting control over his environment, that accompanied the scientific revolution. This process of adaptation had its origins and initial influence in the societies of Western Europe, but in the nineteenth and twentieth centuries these changes have been extended to all other societies and have resulted in a worldwide transformation affecting all human relationships.[4]

But no sooner have we grasped the magnitude of this moment in human history than Black begins a section entitled "The Agony of Modernization." The writer gives only the briefest kind of summary of this agony, but it is clear that he can imagine the horror and the guilt that has accompanied the project.

> ... it is well known that modernization has been accompanied by the greatest calamities that mankind has known. Now that man has perfected weapons capable of destroying all human life, it is unavoidably clear that the problems modernity poses are as great as the opportunities it offers.
>
> Of these problems, one of the most fundamental has been that the construction of a new way of life inevitably involves the destruction of the old. If one thinks of modernization as the integration or the reintegration of societies on the basis of new principles, one must also think of it as involving the disintegration of traditional societies. In a reasonably well-integrated society institutions work effectively, people are in general agreement as to ends and means, and violence and disorder are kept at a low level. When significant and rapid changes are introduced, however, no two elements of a society adapt themselves at the same rate, and the disorder may become so complete that widespread violence breaks out, large numbers of people emigrate, and normal government becomes impossible—all of which has happened frequently in modern times.
>
> Modernization must be thought of, then, as a process that is simultaneously creative and destructive, providing new opportunities and prospects at a high price in human dislocation and suffering. The modern age, more than any other, has been an age of assassinations, of civil, religious, and international wars, of mass slaughter in many forms, and of concentration camps. Never before has human life been disposed of so lightly as the price for immediate goals.[5]

This is the exemplary rhythm of but one out of many such appraisals of the secular project as it exists under the present terms of modernity. Often it is frightening and far from encouraging. But the third Aeschylean moment, the moment of light and some release from burdens ($\mu\alpha\theta$ος) is also present in the process, struggling for emergence. In his own analysis, *Progress and Disillusion*, Raymond Aron has elected a title that is gloomy enough. But I choose one thought from him as I begin to bring my image of secularity to an end. He suggests that a hardheaded form of light or knowledge will attenuate the suffering.

> Men will become less alien to their destiny to the extent that they come to understand it. This does not mean that they will necessarily be less dissatisfied; dissatisfaction, clearly felt, and expressing itself by a desire for definite reform, cannot be called alienation. It is the human response to an order which is, in essence, imperfect.[6]

This is good judgment and a good saying. For what produces alienation is neither the concrete imperfection of it all nor the limits of the act of the imagination which tries to cure it but the absolutism of the lordly mind that cannot tolerate either of these two human things. To what extent it is also this mind that produces the guilt can be one of our final questions.

How can the secular project come closer to innocence?

I propose three different negative elements that have penetrated into the image of secularity. None of these elements belongs to the project but all are deeply associated with it. It is by passing through these things that the secular project always moves toward some approximation to innocence. Approximation is all we want. Anything else would be not only impossible but dangerous.

1. There is a history of painful fantasy that accompanies the self-image of the secular project.

2. There is a life of actual destruction and aggression that accompanies its own image.

3. There is always a tormenting and coexisting set of imitations, parodies, vulgarizations of its own image that fall far short of the truly human and mock the ideal of secularity.

II

Fantasy

By fantasy I mean image elements that have a structural resem-
blance to secularity (and have been identified with it in past versions)
but that really do not belong to it. Thus the secular project thinks of
itself in terms of Prometheanism, Faustianism, rebellion, guilt, separation from God or the world, alienation. The process of fantasy starts
with the first secular act and project of Prometheus. He gave things
to men that belonged to the gods. Secular autonomy is tainted thereafter with fantasies of every manner of defiance and rebellion. These
are the things it appears, in fantasy, to be. The project is not guilty
but appears to be. It is filled with the fantasies of poets like Goethe
as he makes his Prometheus speak to the gods:

> Cover your heavens, O Zeus,
> With cloudy mist
> And like a little boy
> Cutting the heads off thistles,
> Practice your hand
> On oak trees and mountain peaks;
> But you will have to let my earth stand
> And my hut that you did not build,
> And my hearth
> For whose fire
> You envy me.
>
> I know of nothing poorer
> Under the sun than you Gods.
> Wretchedly
> You feed your majesty
> On imposed sacrifices
> And the breath of prayers.

You would waste away
If children and beggars
Were not hopeful fools.

Then the poet turns to the one who is the real Prometheus in this case, one of the great romantic forms of Prometheus in modern history: to his own heart and his consciousness of himself as an artist, as a creator.

Who helped me
Against the pride of the Titans?
Who saved me from death
And slavery?
Did you not do it all alone,
O ardent, holy heart?
. . . .
I honor you? What for?
. . . .

Here I sit, shaping man
After my image,
A race that is like me,
To suffer, to weep,
To rejoice and be glad,
And like myself
To have no regard for you![7]

There are many fine analyses of the fantasy life that has accompanied the secular project. There is Albert Camus's *The Rebel*, Mario Praz's *The Romantic Agony* (especially for the omnipresence of the Satan image), *Totem and Taboo* by Freud. The history of literature is filled with disturbing images of figures who went the way of rebellion or self-assertion. A work that puts history and psychoanalytic theory together to explain one of the first great victories of human culture over such inhibiting fantasies is Saussure's *Le miracle grec*. Perhaps everybody has his own favorite fearful fantasy drawn from a monstrous gothic crowd of villain heroes. Is it Prometheus himself, or Faust, or Icarus, Oedipus the proud solver of riddles, Odysseus, or Manfred, or Captain Ahab, or Ivan Karamazov, Kirilov, some one of the nihilists or anarchists of the nineteenth and twentieth centuries, or Satan in endless shapes? I have noted that in our generation there is increasing use of the figure of Orestes to represent the revolt of man against the religious inhibitions aroused by the secular project. For Orestes faced fantasy and conscience, so one new interpretation goes, to slay his mother and thereby to challenge all the threats and burdens of the superego. This kind of rhetorical and fantasy use of the figure of Orestes by Jean-Paul Sartre in The Flies is too well known to make comment necessary.

Whatever was true of the Greek situation and its obvious ability to take on the project of human thinking and imagining, it is clear in our own case that we have come a long way in learning to proceed on the human path despite the burdens of guilt, fantasy, and feeling. It was a great moment for the secular project when men discovered that these weights of fantasy that are part of the secular reality of man need not cancel the project itself.

It is a good thing that we are learning, because the weight of the fantasy surrounding secularity is very great and not to be minimized by a too facile interpretation of the Bonhoeffer statement that man has come of age. It was not only earlier man who had to go through the experience of a pure image that threatened to be smothered by fantastic distortions of itself. In many ways the secular project still remains a passage through fantastic fire. It is surrounded by the fires of fantasy. We are not as ready for permanent maturity, or as free from the fantasies of man's childhood, as Bonhoeffer thought.

This problem of fantasy is not a game that can be handled by children, nor a mere neo-Gothic entertainment. We now know this about "fantastic" images: They represent very powerful and actual feelings. These images of absolute rebellion, defiance, resentment, alienation, are the fruit of real feelings that are very frightening and very difficult. It was the genius of Aeschylus that he let them come out in full dramatic play. The difficulty is that while some of these feelings are beautiful feelings, some are not, and we would like to disown the latter. Thus we are rather proud of our feelings of rebellion and alienation as we reject the old but struggle for new forms of the secular project. We read Camus's account of these matters with pleasure. But when Lionel Trilling conservatively proposes to us that there are radical elements of resentment, malice, meanness, and the hatred of pleasure in our attack on the old forms and on the middle class, there is no pleasure.[8] We *still have a rather innocent image of our search for innocence.* We prefer to think of the secular project as a beautiful project run exclusively by beautiful people filled with nothing but magnificent feelings.

This is the problematical region where what now emerges as the radical or revolutionary imagination in America must question itself, if it is willing to enter into a dialectical relationship of question and answer with even itself. I have no doubt that certain situations call for a radical act of the imagination and that without it there is no cure for many situations and diseases. Thus the whole true spirit of Christianity, the declaration of the beatitudes, is a radical act of the imagination, demanding a radical transformation of the images of those we think truly blessed and truly powerful. But a radical act of the imagination must not only be radical; it must be truly an act of the imagination. That is to say, it must be able to locate a serious human problem in actuality and provide that vision which is necessary for cure or healing. That is what human beings did when they founded the city of man.

I believe that what the radical imagination is now doing is not radicalizing the imagination, but hystericizing it. It uses various instruments of fantasy and passion, bringing both fantasy and passion to that point of inward intensity at which they no longer represent a reality but do put people in touch with a messianic life of intense imagery and a feeling of salvation. I further mean by this process of hystericizing the imagination (and not really radicalizing it) that it is an act involving the absolute simplification of our images. Its vocabulary, therefore, very much resembles the Newspeak vocabulary of George Orwell in 1984, a vocabulary which, for totalitarian purposes, succeeds in eliminating any truly human form of complexity. It is always right, is arrogantly embarked on the one right way, it is not to be questioned, and its demands are nonnegotiable. Such an intensity of fantasy, purpose, and passion is so canalized into one or two images that the process superficially resembles a truly radical act of the imagination. It limits human conversation, thought and feeling to a few areas—which we can call a package deal. Above all, it perpetually challenges and exacerbates the consciences of the surrounding world, demanding that they be for or against, but for or against in terms of the limitations it has authoritatively placed on the discussion. It is especially tragic when the campus imagination, the university imagination—one of whose great functions should eternally be to distinguish between the radical and the hysterical imagination—should itself begin to succumb to the life of exacerbated, blown up, hysterical image.

As it tries to imagine the secular project in some adequate way, the imagination often finds itself polarized between two sets of hysterical fantasy, on the right and on the left, in fierce simplicity and in fierce battle with each other. The secular project is no longer a project but a battle between opposing fantasies. The spectacular becomes a substitute for the passage through the totally human. Fantasy takes the place of the imagination.

It is not by any means the intention of the mass media to conspire toward the further aggravation of this situation. But that is the way it works out. It is true that the new electronic age, especially the age of television, is so much beginning to unite the world (after its fashion) that we do take on the shape of a global village. The trouble is that the mass media make us a global village in too many senses. They tend to make the nations and the world a global village in the order of fantasy and feeling, so that at any one moment we are caught, all of us, in a small pocket of a handful of images and events. All our energies are invited into a literal *village* of the imaginative and emotional life. The result is a vast narrowing of the idea of the important and the idea of the human, as well as the narrowing of the life of fantasy. This is a process which lends itself more to the emergence of the hysterical imagination than a truly radical imagination. The new Left has taken full advantage of this structural parallel to create a special version of fantasy life about the present status of the secular project. That it is always nearly right (like hysteria itself) is part of the explanation for its success in creating hysteria in our fantastic life. But this is only a modern example of the *fantastic* difficulties that are being regularly suffered by the secular project.

American liberalism is another force that might yet seize the moment creatively in the midst of the darkness. But American liberalism, it seems to me, has similar, though of course less extreme, difficulties as it is trapped again and again into a narrowing of the imagination, an intensification of fantasy, and a failure to pursue the true range of the secular project, all of which result from the polarizing of the imagination. The liberal imagination becomes obsessively preoccupied with the Right; it constructs a package deal of four or five social and political items, and a large part of its purpose is narrow self-identification and unity against the opposing force. Both groups fall into rigid systems that, I repeat, are more marked, in their imagining, by relations over against each other than by the pursuit of some objective reality which we might without hesitation associate with the secular project.

In the case of liberalism, one very critical effect of this polarization has been a fairly complete neglect of the relationship of this country to the vast undeveloped regions of Asia, Africa, and Latin America. When a thing is not imagined, it is as though it is not there for us. Thus Asia, Africa, and Latin America have become simply not there, despite the intensity of the interest in parts of Asia through the war. Since the inception of our programs of foreign aid, there never has been such a rock bottom level of interest and economic aid. As I write these lines, there has just been another decisive reduction of a half billion dollars in the foreign aid bill, and all this without protestations of any kind. Yet here would be, I would think, a most solemn vocation of true liberalism to the outer world, and a true core for the secular and human project.

Thus polarization, and the fantasies that go with it, inhibit imagining, as also they inhibit the project. An occasional voice is heard. Senator Edmund S. Muskie warned, in a speech to the International Development Conference in Washington, that "the survival of the democratic process and of man himself" might come to depend on whether the country is willing to increase its help to the poor nations of the world.[9] Two days later the *Times* published a vigorous editorial on the subject, but the subject is hardly steady news for either the *Times* or the rest of the national press. Nor am I aware that the universities have made any serious educational contribution to the idea of development, though education is the central need for this idea. The universities want to become relevant and are on the catastrophic brink of politicizing themselves. Yet here is a subject in terms of which they could, with vision, become completely relevant at the same time that they might warn of the serious danger of politicizing or colonializing or imperializing the issue or the situation. The irony is that if they were to assert themselves in this educational task, teaching us to keep political and imperial fantasy (or fact) out of this part of our project, they would themselves be learning how to be relevant (while using the powerful instruments of the life of the mind) without destroying themselves with the fantasies (or fact) of politicization. Here I recommend the reading of the report on development aid made to the President of the United States by a sixteen-member task force on foreign aid headed by Rudolph A. Peterson.[10] That document proposes two very concrete ways as examples of the purification of our objectives. First it warns that all our development programs should be independent of all military and even economic programs that provide "assistance for security purposes." Secondly, it proposes that the major channel for our help should be international lending organizations and not our own national institutions. These and other features of the report are good examples of that kind of detailed vision which also helps to free our images from all the opposing fantasies of imperialism or colonialism. But polarization makes it almost impossible for the nations to set out on this great, objective path.

III

Aggression

If the search for innocence is made difficult by the life of fantasy, how much more difficult does it become in the face of the line of *actual* and destructive aggression which has always accompanied the history of secularity. Again this capacity for destruction is not identical with the secular project; but it has always accompanied it, and it is only with the greatest effort that we can dissociate the one from the other. It is an example of the counterimage and of the painful dramatic processes that move the human imagination from negative to positive images.

Secularity now passes through this process not abstractly but in a set of concrete contemporary situations, in all of which the human spirit is trying to separate the drive forward from the destructive drive, the energy from the hatred. If we were to review the violent polarizations of party spirit in the United States in the last several years, it would be clear that we have been radically divided as to whether or not we have been engaged, throughout the world, in a positive or destructive national policy. The dilemma has not been philosophical or purely speculative; on the contrary it has been enough to produce a national agony of spirit and a dangerous polarization of national opinion. Unfortunately this is only a lesser incident among all the modern forms of the problem. For we of the last three generations are tormented by our inability to vomit the hate out of the secularity. We have been in the midst of a great renaissance of human energy and genius. But we have also been in the midst of the terrors of our own violence, to a degree that seems beyond the reach of the human imagination at its very worst. There have been two world wars of incredible dimensions. What was done to the Jews at Dachau and Belsen in the years of the Second World War seemed to defy possibility and to defy any reaching beyond it. Now we know with a wild instinctual sense that we can transcend even this and can destroy everything. But we do not quite know yet that we can wish this and actually want it, as permanent co-element in the drive toward secularity. Here we are still in the primitive stage of projecting all these possibilities on systems, on establishments, on governments, on the political order. We are still projecting our own possibilities in a total way onto these outside forces and villains and are still slow to face the basic discovery that there is a wish behind a thought. Naturally the secular project finds it hard to confront all of its wishes and its hates. But the evidence is becoming clearer and clearer; it is only the endless ability of man to defend himself against self-knowledge that prevents the obvious confrontation of secularity with its own evil and that slows its dramatic passage toward its own idea.

But we are becoming more conscious.

A fascinating development in modern scholarship is the study of aggression, notably of group aggression. Dr. Nicholas Tinbergen, new Oxford professor of animal behavior, warned in his inaugural address that the fate of the world may depend on the outcome of this growing research. The work of Konrad Lorenz in Austria is perhaps best known because of the publicity attached to his book *On Aggression*, though it is doubtful if his work is the most important. There is a French Institute of Polemology (in Paris), and there is a polemological institute at Groningen in the Netherlands. There is an important development in England, at the University of Sussex, under the leadership of the English historian Norman Cohn. It is a Center for Research in Collective Psychopathology. There are the studies of violence by our own national commissions. Nor must we forget that a great part of the literature of psychoanalytic theory is in fact a study of aggression.

Indeed, the march of secularity toward its own idea is no game for children (I have come a long way from the first step in my own image). It is a game mixed with horror. Today the fear of the horror is found everywhere. We remember that it even creeps into the pure idea of the pure mind of the pure scientist who has invented new power and cannot get rid of the suffering that goes with it. He tries to tell himself that he represents the pure and innocent, the perfect secular idea, and that it is the political order alone which by war and hate fouls the nest of the beautiful idea. He storms against the political order, reviles it, uses every projective resource to conceal from himself our basic fact that the idea and image of secularity is a dramatic image which he too must pass through in suffering. The political order has been corrupt a thousand times and the intellectual, writer, artist, has always risen against it. One hopes this will always be the case. But it is another matter to claim politics as the corrupt body of a pure and innocent intellectual idea. This kind of absolutizing of innocence and guilt leads to the polarization which increasingly characterizes American society. From start to finish it is a Cartesian separation between mind and body, between innocence and guilt. This form of innocence is a dangerous thing and can become a savage thing. The intelligence too can become savage.

IV

The Nonhuman

We come to the last of the counterimages of secularity which we must pass through. It is that image of the secular life which is closed off from imagination, from vision, from value, from commitment, and from the sacred. This has been the classical denunciatory image of the secular. It has included the image of the world as pure machine, in motion indeed, but without even a reason for its motions. This is a picture of what I chose to call the "demythologized" secular world. But I recall to memory that when I think of the secular world as "demythologized" I am not saying in some overly definite way that it has lost its points of transcendental and symbolic reference; I am more generally concerned with those reductive processes which take all capacity for vision, imagination, and humanity out of the secular project.

Here is a crux of our agonizing over the nature of the secular image. We must not minimize the burden of fantasy and the burden of actual aggression. But these, at their very worst, have something awesome about them; they are a more tolerable burden than that the unconditionality and redemptive vision of secularity should be reduced to the tawdry, the cheap, the dehumanized, the closed off thing that is separate from meaning and the human. At this moment it is increasingly difficult to endure this confusing of the true image of the secular project with a fraudulent imitation.

Our mistake was to have admitted the possibility of a "demythologized" and mechanical level of existence for secularity. Once you accept this abstraction and this level as a possibility you are in a trap from which there is no exit. And when we say that there is no way out of self-enclosed secularity, it may be this third and tawdry image which has taken hold of the imagination. I believe that Whitehead is right when he says that this idea should never have been admitted as an idea and that even now it should not be accepted as a basis for philosophical speculation.

There is, then, this first drive in secularity toward the nonhuman, a drive toward the totally mechanical and the totally technological. Actually, it is as though a great debate and a great and polarized battle is going on among us between the purely mechanical and the free human spirit. Stated in these bald terms, it is a contest between the nonhuman and the human. The street forms of the battle are easily visible. What is not so visible is the debate as it occurs, not in some simplistic version of a battle between the intellectuals and the middle class, but in and at the heart of the modern intelligence itself. I take up the beautiful book of a distinguished anthropologist and writer, Loren Eiseley, called *The Unexpected Universe* and without difficulty I pick up the pieces that describe these contesting drives. On the one hand he describes the danger of the mechanical construction of the human:

> All past civilizations have been localized and have had, there-fore, the divergent mutative quality to which we have referred. They have offered choices to men. Ideas have been exchanged, along with technological innovations, but never on so vast, over-whelming and single-directed a scale as in the present. Increasingly, *there is but one way into the future* [italics mine]: the technological way. The frightening aspect of this situation lies in the constriction of human choice. Western technology has released irrevocable forces, and the one world that has been talked about so glibly is simply a distraught conformity produced by the centripetal forces of Western society. So great is its power over men that any other solution, any other philosophy, is silenced. Men, unknowingly, and whether for good or ill, appear to be making their last decisions about human destiny. To pursue the biological analogy, it is as though, instead of many adaptive organisms, a single gigantic ani-mal embodied the only organic future of the world.[11]

My own thought was that here we have almost a parody, in the order of actual life, of the mechanical universe of Newton, the reign through the late eighteenth and early nineteenth centuries of the balanced world machine and universal order, perfect organization and clockwork, everything under a vast law and equilibrium.

This is the nonhuman picture which Eiseley himself, and so many others, now rejects. It is because he conceives the nature of reality itself to be radically different that he writes a book called *The Unexpected Universe*. Because he is a learned student of Darwin, he begins to describe the new image of the universe in the following way:

> Only later did we begin to realize that what Charles Darwin had introduced into nature was not Newtonian predictability, but absolute random novelty. Life was bent, in the phrase of Alfred Russel Wallace, upon "infinite departure." No living thing, not even man, understood upon what journey he had embarked. Time was no longer cyclic or monotonously repetitious. It was historic, novel, and unreturning. Since that momentous discovery, man has, whether or not he realizes or accepts his fate, been moving in a world of contingent forms.[12]

Then the images of contingency and novelty and difference begin to pour forth in the language of a rich prose style. It is easy to rest content with being frightened by this new world, but it is better to remember that in the end it is a more human world, justifying the identity and differences (I have said *the unconditionality*) of each one of us, each history, each moment:

> . . . the earth's atmosphere of oxygen appears to be the product of a biological invention, photosynthesis, another random event that took place in Archeozoic times. . . . The brain of man, that strange gray iceberg of conscious and unconscious life, was similarly unpredictable until its appearance. . . . likeness in body has, paradoxically, had to diversify in thought. . . .
>
> Einstein is reputed to have once remarked that he refused to believe that God plays at dice with the universe. But as we survey the long backward course of history, it would appear that in the phenomenal world the open-endness of time is unexpectedly an essential element of his creation. Whenever an infant is born, the dice, in the shape of genes and enzymes and the intangibles of chance environment, are being rolled again. . . . a strange unexpectedness lingers about our world. . . .
>
> Contingency has escaped into human hands and flickers unseen behind every whirl of our machines, every pronouncement of political policy.[13]

So much for the purely mechanical as major part of the non-human image of man and the beginnings of a different vision, a transformation of the evidence, that must begin to assert itself in more human images.

Above all, it should never have been permitted to be separated from the human. The secular as nonhuman vacuum has now become the most unbearable part of its negative image—and the source of much of its guilt. In what ways it must be human becomes the fundamental question.

It is not a matter of rejecting autonomy or unconditionality or modernization. I think that it is impossible and absurd to reject modernization. It is the poor who will suffer most and do suffer most from any attack on or absence of modernization. The revolution that today attacks modernization without qualification and without imagination is a reactionary and puritanical movement. But what is required is the restoration of the smaller human line, in as many forms as possible, within the necessarily massive lines of the new project.

If we return to Black's definition of modernization, we will see that it is really a one-sided definition. It calls for the adjustment of man and his institutions to the new revolution in human knowledge and resource. But this definition (in an otherwise very human book) does not call for the constant adjustment of modernity to the human.

If the better way of studying the split between the sacred and the secular was to regard these two forces as elements of the same human consciousness, then the same method should be followed in studying the relations between the great line and the smaller human line in the secular project (and in that latest phase of it we call modernity). It is man who creates the massive quality and the elements of infinite power, organization, communication, precision, efficiency; it is man who struggles with these things (or does not struggle adequately) to give them what can really be called humanity. By a supreme irony it is his own talents and ideas, his own enormous energy and planning, that becomes the latest form of the cosmological with which he must struggle (but often does not).

So the two drives are two historical forces but they are also two forces in the one man.

By itself the force that leads toward the great achievements of modernity is a lumbering, towering, mechanical giant that will lead to disaster if allowed to operate on its own isolated laws. We have only to look again at the very largest and most crucial element in the picture to see that this is so. After thousands of years the secular project, and after several hundred years the process of modernization, remains a phenomenon of the western world. If left to itself the same process will continue to divide the developed and the undeveloped worlds—the rich and the poor—in a way that I have said can only lead to catastrophe. The problem is to be located where the medieval moralists located the greatest of the vices: in that acedia, or indifference, or passivity on the part of this other element in us which is meant to control and direct what we have been calling "history." At the moment there is the crisis and the guilt of passivity toward the international poor.

There are many ways in which this acedia, this passivity, works within that part of us which ought to be struggling to give human shape to the secular project. The temptation of the artist has always been to build another and a better world, completely outside this present world, this "world he never made." The temptation of the American poet has been to go off in a corner and write poetry within which he can feel beautifully sorry for himself. The temptation of many other writers has been the temptation to self-mockery and self-parody, on the ground that today the imagination is helpless and can really do nothing over against this giant new world of reality. For others the acedia is excused by history, a concept of a history-outside-of-us which has been severely dealt with by Karl Popper in his *The Open Society and Its Enemies*:

> Neither nature nor history can tell us what we ought to do. Facts, whether those of nature or those of history, cannot make the decision for us, they cannot determine the ends we are going to choose. It is we who introduce purpose and meaning into nature and into history. . . .
>
> This dualism of facts and decisions is, I believe, fundamental. Facts as such have no meaning; they can gain it only through our decisions. Historicism is only one of many attempts to get over this dualism; it is born of fear, for it shrinks from realizing that we bear the ultimate responsibility even for the standards we choose. But such an attempt seems to me to represent precisely what is usually described as superstition. For it assumes that we can reap

where we have not sown; it tries to persuade us that if we merely fall into step with history everything will and must go right, and that no fundamental decision on our part is required; it tries to shift our responsibility on to history, and thereby on the play of demoniac powers beyond ourselves; it tries to base our actions upon the hidden intentions of these powers, which can be revealed to us only in mystical inspirations and intuitions; and it thus puts our actions and ourselves on the moral level of a man who, inspired by horoscopes and dreams, chooses his lucky number in a lottery. Like gambling, historicism is born of our despair in the rationality and responsibility of our actions. It is a debased hope and a debased faith, an attempt to replace the hope and the faith that springs from our moral enthusiasm and the contempt for success by a certainty that springs from a pseudo-science; a pseudo-science of the stars, or of "human nature," or of historical destiny.[14]

The history we are so afraid of is a creation of man. The giant nonhuman elements of the modern secular project have been made by ourselves. As the last word of my image I repeat that it is man who has fashioned this latest form of the cosmological before which he feels so helpless.

We are in the intermediate stage of suffering. We are in the trap.

But there is a stage beyond. There is the possibility of a new hypothesis. We are permanently committed, for all time, not like Sisyphus but with hope, to that permanent search.

This is the end of my attempt at a sketch of secularity within which the religious imagination might be able to live and breathe. It began as world of autonomy and independent rationality. It quickly became a human and an anthropological rather than a cosmological image. The image went further and further in its refusal to be mechanical. It discovered it contained a world of good and evil, some contest of some kind between some forms of what St. Paul called *principalities and powers*. It discovered the dimension not of disgust but terror. It became a permanent march toward more and more light.

Some people have even told me I was writing about the sacred.

That would not be a problem for me so long as I would have convinced a good number of people that I had been talking legitimately about the secular. But now I wish to write an epilogue on some of the relations of the sacred and secular within the life and breath of this image.

EPILOGUE

The Reconciliation

If I am rightly asked what are the consequences of such an image of the secular order as we have now constructed—what are its practical as well as its theoretical consequences—my reaction is that we must rephrase the question and then limit it.

1. Let me rephrase the question. I prefer to ask what are the consequences and especially the practical consequences we *should* be aiming at in the construction of new religious images of the secular order. I hope my own extended image gets somewhere with some of them. But it is only one image; the tasks that are set before the religious imagination by the new range of secularity are so serious and ambitious that they call not for one image but for the creation of a multitude of new images by many people.

2. Let me delimit the question of consequences. The consequences we would wish to bring about by new ways of imagining secularity are so large and serious that any one essay on the subject should try to work within some narrow limit.

After mentioning a few general issues I will discuss the relevance of my own image-making to the specific question within which this book was born. That question was: How can we restore an inner unity to the divided religious imagination of our day, racked as it is by living in a narrow religious corner and a huge secular world?

I

A Few General Issues

One great consequence, on the broad level of history and institutions, that our new images of secularity must aim at is a reconciliation between Christianity and the Enlightenment, the forces of the intelligence and faith, the great historical forces of the sacred and the secular. The gap is still there. What could be more important than that these two forces should work together against every form of the nonhuman in our civilization? The religious imagination should explore the hypothesis that precisely this is the central task of secularity.

True secularity has more often been an attack on inhuman forms of the cosmological than it has been an attack on religion. I repeat that we ought to experiment with a reading of much of the history of the secular project as a series of attacks on intolerable, nonhuman forms of the cosmological. If secularity were to find in religion a form of the cosmological that is not a threat to man, a form that would instead be foundation and guarantee of the project, then history might reach another significant milestone—a milestone of collaboration with old religious enemies and an end to some of the painful divisions of the intelligence in our culture.

Consider an extraordinary factor within the secularity of our own time. It comes down to this, that if we seek the consequence of collaboration through new images, then we should realize that this is also happening in the secular order: New images of itself are arising within secularity itself. Our own dramatic, human, and free image of the secular project seems to me to be the very image the intelligence is now proposing to itself as a definition of the work that lies before it. It has veered sharply away from mechanistic and nonhuman images of its project. It is filled with remarkable moral earnestness. It wants to be on the side of every really human revolution. It begins to describe itself not merely as the mind but as the conscience of the nation. It is critical of every form of mechanical imperialism, mechanical organization. It does not wish to be alienated from politics and therefore invents the new politics. It is in horror at the evil in the world. In a word, it is now rejecting its own mechanistic and "demythologized" image of itself. If all this is not happening in theory it is happening in fact. There is also a new Prometheanism lodged in much of this new image. But to screen it out of the new project is the new task. The argument of this whole book takes that for granted.

There is another fact of the gravest import for the religious imagination, a fact that can produce decisive consequences in the whole inner fabric of that imagination for generations to come. At an early stage of my argument I suggested that there were people who, in the name of relevance, were ready to give up Christ, to "demythologize" Christiantity, were ready to give up all the special historical and imaginative resources of the Christian in order to deal with the world on its own terms. The irony of this decision would be that it would present us with a confrontation between a pygmy and a giant that had decided to recover its identity. They would settle for a little Christ over against a great if purified Prometheus. The prime consequence I, for one, would aim at in reimagining the secular as I have is to contribute to preventing the religious imagination from making so mad a decision. If secularity is not so mad why should we be? I hope to make the point clearer as I move through this epilogue. In the meantime it all comes down to this, that every part of the Word of Christianity as well as its historical reality was meant to be an instrument to deal with the dignity, the power, and the horror of the world. It is only our recovered image of secularity that will prevent a stupid form of reductionism in the religious imagination. If the latter does not seek and find its own full identity it will not become a significant factor in the building of identities in the world. *In a word a truly realistic image of secularity will as a consequence prevent the reduction of the religious imagination to anything less than itself.* This must be especially true of our image of Christ.

If this turns out to be true my own image of the secular world will have come full circle. For the very first element that I proposed in any new religious imagining of secularity was a kind of descent into hell which would strip every religious and Christian form from the world; the descent would mean a firm acceptance of the unconditioned and autonomous images of the world. This means that we begin with the most basic supposition of secularity and that no later stage of this image abandons it. But now the final irony begins: In order to produce this very consequence, in order to help the world become what it is, in order to deal with the magnitude and terror thereof, the religious imagination must summon all its own resources.

We will be looking in more detail at this phenomenon of full circle. My method here has been an imitation of the method of Plato in *The Republic*. We remember that in *The Republic* the argument asks the good man to strip himself of everything but his goodness; he is asked to give up everything else that might cloud the discussion of the question: Is goodness worthwhile for its own sake or only for the sake of all those things, from good fortune to reputation, that traditionally have come with it? The method is pushed to the point of putting the man on the cross as sole external recompense for his goodness. It is only after goodness has won its interior and constitutive victory, on its own terms, that Plato allows another truth to emerge. All that had been lost comes rushing back; to have given them up was the condition of not losing them. The friends come trooping back, and the peace, the good fortune, the reputation, even the worldly prosperity. Thus the tenth book of *The Republic* ends where the first book began, though on different terms of possession.

This is what we want to make happen to the religious imagination. It must give up its own forms in the secular world. This it must do as first step toward the redemption of our new world. It must take the secular risk. But as further exploration leads to deeper knowledge of the complete identity of this world, its magnitude, dignity and horror (and the true dimensions of the task of redemption), the religious imagination will have to rediscover its own complete identity in order to deal with it. That will not be in order to impose itself and its forms as master, even as master of meaning, but to serve the world as servant in the tortuous search of the world for identity and salvation.

To recall in this way the true dimensions of secularity and the secular project and thus to refuse to demythologize the world does not at all mean that we now opt for an apocalyptic and mystical, an evangelical vision of secularity which would cancel out or obscure every other quality and dimension within its project. Our image of secularity is composed of various "moments" which do not cancel one another out. If therefore, there is a realistic possibility of horror within the secular—which we must fight against and not conspire with—this in no way affects that moment in which mathematics (and every art and science) has its own calm and unconditional reality. On the other hand we must remember that while nothing can take its own life from mathematics, this first moment can be put at the service of the later moments of the human, or of good and evil, or of horror. But even in the moment of horror nothing in heaven or on earth can change that exact form of redemption which belongs to the order and the moment of mathematics.

II

Specific Consequences

These are large issues. They are too large to be dealt with except by hope and continued striving. I turn to a more limited frame of consequence. My own limited question is large, but it is specific.

I want to return to where I began. I began by proposing that the religious imagination was in a state of crisis, that it was in sore need of an image of secularity within which it could live, breathe and work; it was living a divided life between two worlds, the sacred and the secular. Could it accept secularity and take the secular risk without self-betrayal? Could it reject secularity without saying farewell to the city of man? Clearly it has chosen to enter the city and has placed some vague blessing on "the project." But it is in the divided state of entrance without acceptance. This is the limited frame within which I wished to do most of my own imagining. We aim, that is, at the consequence of helping to conquer division in the imaginations of all those who have had to lead a double, torn life of sacred and secular.

We have tended to bury the whole enormous divided situation of the imagination in the unconscious. At any rate, where the situation *is* looked at it has become axiomatic that the division we are addressing ourselves to is a division in principle as well as in fact. I pick up a book like *A Rumor of Angels* by a fine sociologist like Peter Berger and he argues that a pluralistic (divided) culture of divided roles, religious and nonreligious, is at the center of the religious plausibility crisis. I do not think I am unfair in saying that secularity as obstacle and unhappy development for the religious consciousness is the basic assumption here. And I listen to Bryan Wilson (author of *Sects and Society* and *Religion in Secular Society*) as he tells us that the religious consciousness grows and thrives in stable communities of "known" people, and there lay the strength of past Christianity. Now that *other* organizational forms break in upon this defining element, he tells us, they corrupt this unified and basic idea. A central supposition for him is that secular concerns, or what have always been interpreted as the nonreligious elements of consciousness, cannot be assimilated by the truly religious consciousness.

The basic image behind this kind of thinking—and indeed it has been a typical self-image of the religious imagination—is that there is a narrow abiding part of the consciousness that is religious and makes sense, but that for the rest there is sheer fact, or whirl is king, or contingency, or vacuity.

The fortunate thing is that our instincts are often better than our theories or formal decisions. By instinct the religious imagination is already undergoing a new and unprecedented diaspora. This diaspora of Christians into the world is itself a new revolution in the Church, just as the diaspora of human beings into wider and wider worlds is one of the great revolutionary characteristics of "modernization." It is passing decisively into the secular world and therefore into new forms. But it holds desperately to its own inner quarrels. It would be at greater peace if it could articulate the reasons and forge the images which would help it do all that it must now do. It must move out.

A COMMON LOGIC

There will be less division in the religious imagination if it discovers the possibility of a common logic of unconditionality and redemption in the sacred and the secular. It is the possibility of such a common logic that I have had in mind from the very first stage of my own image of secularity. I was looking for some master analogy between the two orders that would not abandon the unconditionality and autonomy of the secular and that would not betray the sacred. We need a logic that will relate and differentiate the secular and the sacred.

Let us go back to the word *identity* and the companion word *emergence*. We decided that what has identity can be located in itself and distinguished from everything else. Emergence is any process by which things move into such identity and differentiation. Other central words I have been using relate easily to this fundamental vocabulary. The idea of unconditionality for everything in the secular order simply means that the elements of this order move toward a self-contained existence that is not constitutively conditioned by anything outside of itself. The word *autonomy* has the same meaning. These are all important words. But they will serve their purpose better if we will remember that they are not absolutes. They have a history; they have connotations and meanings which come from their history and usage; they must choose the connotations they want and the connotations they do not want. For example, the movement toward identity and differentiation in everything and everybody does not necessarily connote hostility in any way, nor does it connote isolation and unrelatedness. Identity can be related to every manner of generalizing theory. It is not a solitary atomic fact, for identities (and their "meanings") emerge within contexts and patterns and relationships. Nor does identity here mean that two things are identical if they share a common form or that the sacred and the secular share a common logic in *this* sense. This would give the secular a constitutively conditional existence, whereas our hypothesis has been that God does not require *this* relationship and has gone much further in ceding the unconditional possession of selfhood to the world. The deepest relationship is the sharing of inward life.

Let us ask how this vocabulary can describe a common logic

between sacred and secular and thus contribute to dissolving the divisions in the imagination.

THE SACRED

The sacred is par excellence the inner life, the absolute self-possession and self-identity of God. In simple summary it is said, "Who is like unto God?" The religious imagination has fought a long struggle to separate God out from everything else in the world while keeping him altogether present to the world. The central history of the whole of the Old Testament is a separating out of God from all other gods and from all idols. The idea and location of the sacred as divine self-possession—to the point of adoration of that which reaches such a point of internality and selfhood—becomes absolutely clear. God tells the Jewish people who He is: "I am that I am." "Thus shalt thou say to the children of Israel, I AM hath sent me unto you." There are many other givings of an absolute name and an absolute identity to God. "Before me there was no God, neither shall there be after me. I, even I, am the Lord and beside me there is no savior . . . I am the first and the last, and beside me there is no God." And the consequences are clear for the heart as well as for the mind: "Hear, O Israel, the Lord our God is our Lord, and thou shalt love the Lord thy God with all thy heart and with all thy soul and with all thy might."

Everything else that is specifically sacred is sacred in a secondary sense, and in relationship to *this* marvelous identity of God: the Law, the sacred vessels, the temple, the city of Jerusalem, the priesthood, the sacrifice, the ark of the covenant, the sacred calendar of the year, the great feasts, the pasch, the prayers. This secondary order of the sacred had as its first purpose the formal declaration and honoring of the divine identity. There are other looser and wider forms of the sacred. But there has always been this specific form which has had as its vocation the role of declaring the prime specificity of God. He is spoiled by nothing; He is confused with nothing else; no taint or confusion enters into him. That accounts for his eminent holiness and goodness. But this does not preclude such a God from being infinitely outgoing, full of love, responsive, historical. Indeed, this is the unique quality of the God of Israel that the one existence in no way precludes the other:

1. He is what He is, an absolute principle of identity, the God of complete inner life, and father of every other specificity in the universe.

2. But it is also as though He has put on the mind of man, engaging in a covenant with him, a God of promises, demander of fidelity, angry, jealous of his people, making specific decisions, committing himself to events, peoples, individuals, offering reconciliation. He is an action.

There is no contradiction between this form of inwardness and this form of outwardness; the outwardness is really a set of historical demands that first Israel, and after Israel the world, should share his inwardness and identity, and not let itself be dissolved by forces counter to and destructive of real life. It is a strange thing, not to be able to understand the God of the Old Testament. What do we want, a beautiful God?

In order that the absolute identity of the Living God beyond and in the world be really grasped it was necessary to separate out a whole people who would be given this historical task of the identification of the sacred. For such a role it was necessary not that Israel be integrated into other peoples but that it be sorted out. In fact it may have been necessary that some far from perfect consequences follow for this solitary people in order that it accomplish that which was altogether vital to the history of man. It may have been necessary that from Egypt to Sion to Babylon this nation should have a lonely identity to the point of theocratic rigidity, at times to the point of a ritual smothering, in order that there should never be complete forgetfulness of the task at hand:

> And Moses went up to God: and the Lord called unto him from the mountain, and said: Thus shalt thou say to the house of Jacob, and tell the children of Israel: You have seen what I have done to the Egyptians, how I have carried you upon the wings of eagles, and have taken you to myself. If therefore you will hear my voice, and keep my covenant, you shall be my peculiar possession above all people: for all the earth is mine. And you shall be to me a priestly kingdom, and a holy nation. These are the words thou shalt speak to the children of Israel. [Exod. 19:3–6]

The same separation and sorting out occurs with a chosen set of individuals who have a special role in the great task of Israel and who seem, so sharp is their own emergence, to share in the remarkable identity, the separateness, the self-possession of God himself. Of these Abraham is the first great model of a theology that is both communal at heart and is at the same time carving out the sharpest kind of individuations among men. So we read that:

> The Lord said to Abraham: Go forth out of thy country, and from thy kindred, and out of thy father's house, and come into the land which I shall shew thee. And I will make of thee a great nation. [Gen. 12:1–2]

And on another occasion Abraham said to Lot:

> Let there be no quarrel, I beseech thee, between me and thee, and between my herdsmen and your herdsmen: for we are brethren. Behold the whole land is before thee: depart from me I pray thee: if thou wilt go to the left hand, I will take the right: if thou choose the right hand, I will pass to the left. . . . And Lot chose to himself the country about the Jordan, and he departed from the east: and they were separated one brother from the other. [Gen. 13:8–11]

Thus Abraham takes on a progressive identity which will fit him to be the forger of a people.

There are a few pages in *The Idea of the Holy* of Rudolf Otto that I have found particularly helpful here. They seem to me to come very close to proposing an ultimate relationship between the marvelous identity and inner unconditionality in anything and the idea of the holy itself. As a thinker Otto is a strong believer that one must become a master of the rational before becoming a master of mystery, and within the order of mystery he is no particular believer in the spurious forms of excitement that come from "the merely strange, the extraordinary, the marvelous, and the fantastic." All these things are "a mere substitute for the genuine thing."[1] What attracts him are the striking, complex, and unique ways in which the world gathers itself together into a fact, as though an infinite set of relations had succeeded in saying something. For his examples Otto goes to that place in the Book of Job where God himself is conducting a self-defense that is meant to still the doubts of Job. He does not try to overwhelm his creature; rather He moves toward an "inward convincement" that comes from what I will here call the evidence of identities, each one of which is a precise thing fleshed in an environment and in its own inner life, no one of which is stretching toward a vast teleology or demonstration of power.

There is the eagle, that "dwelleth and abideth on the rock, upon the crag of the rock, and the strong place"; her "eyes behold afar off" her prey and her "young ones also suck up blood, and where the slain are, there is she."

Otto points out that the examples can even demonstrate a striking *lack of wisdom* (it is hard to think of any book on natural theology that would demonstrate God's ways this way). Thus in the case of the ostrich:

> Which leaveth her eggs in the earth, and warmeth them in the dust, and forgetteth that the foot may crush them or that the wild beast may break them. She is hardened against her young ones as though they were not hers: her labour is in vain without fear; because God hath *deprived her of wisdom*, neither hath he imparted to her *understanding*.[2]

And so it is with the "wild ass" and the unicorn, the "wild goat" and the hind, and with the greater examples of the hippopotamus (behemoth) and crocodile (leviathan).

Otto finally suggests what is for him the point of a theodicy given by God himself. It is not merely that these things, these identities, are beyond all thought and by us inconceivable (such things would strike Job dumb but not convince him inwardly). No, but "That of which we are conscious is rather an *intrinsic value* in the incomprehensible—a value inexpressible, positive, and 'fascinating.'"[3]

What we can say, then, is that the God of Abraham, Isaac, and Jacob, is a principle of inward life. This is one central way in which the religious imagination must see what is *behind* the world and what is or should be *in* the world. Thus it can imagine the sacred and the secular according to a common logic. Our image of the secular said that everything should have or should come into its own life. Therefore the sacred would be faithless to itself if it did not appear as ground and creator, model and origin, of secularity thus conceived.

Thus conceived, secularity becomes an order of salvation and redemption for all things. But this salvation can never neglect the contextual body of culture, society, and history.

We can be especially aware of what this means if we bring these images of identity and emergence to the human world. What human beings seem to hunger for at all costs is a sense of self-possession that is the same thing as the good taste of self. Nor is this a selfish phrase, for it also includes the good taste of otherness. Nor is it merely a pious phrase; rather it is one that gives substance and actuality to the evangelical ideas of redemption and salvation. For there seems today to be a special need for this taste of the actual existence of the self. In fact one could bring together all the forms of the cosmological images of the world in this book under the single rubric that they are all enemies of or obstacles to identity, salvation, the good taste of self. Whether it is the new cosmology in which man seems a point in the infinite dark, or the new endless proliferation of objects, or the development of overpowering forms of mechanical organization, or the drives of revolution that have lost contact with the imagination, all these things are imaged as enemies of the possession of self.

As for this precise moment in the history of the United States, it is increasingly clear, indeed it is becoming strikingly clear in what new direction very powerful sets of feelings choose to go: They choose to go in the direction of reclaiming the self in many concrete social ways. There are literally hundreds of movements toward participatory democracy, toward the creation of situations within which the individual can be heard in the group. There is the beginning of a return toward regionalism in government. There is a new respect in the air for more parochial ways of running things over against the universalistic and centralistic images that have been so dear to American liberalism. The black man, at least for this historical moment, declares against integration and against the loss of his own culture and his own differences. The many ethnic groups are beginning to reemerge as solid and proud ways of living life. This may mean that their language and their cultural identities will reemerge with them. Students are fighting on the campuses for participatory existence. Community groups want to be in charge of their own schools. The states want a large part of federal taxes to be returned to them for the spending thereof. All of this may sound completely anarchic, and the competition between rival emergences will very unhappily produce some catastrophes. But it is far from the completely anarchic; it means the reemergence of articulated social realities and groups without which the individual cannot find identity or salvation.[4]

UNITY AND SEPARATION

We must not only remember that the secular project of man lives within the same logic and image as the sacred. It is also precisely this logic which preserves the identity of, and the absolute difference between, the sacred and the secular. The two also have their *separate* identities.

The preservation of this difference need be no cause of division in the imagination. In fact, if we do not preserve the principle of absolute identity and difference from everything else in the inward life of God and therefore at the very heart of the universe, we will see that principle crumble away and dissolve at every other point in the universe.

To help me get hold of the meaning of this statement I go back to a remarkable and central scene in *The Stranger* of Camus. In a blazing, tormenting sun which is itself dissolving all differences, the Stranger shoots and kills an Arab. But as he pulls the trigger he is seized with a feeling of what we can call metaphysical indifference: He feels that to pull the trigger or not to pull the trigger is one and the same thing.

The power of *The Stranger* comes largely from its sharp studies of various forms and moods of non-difference and in-difference in the world. As though the principle of identity did not matter and was not present in the universe. The book ends with the hero shaking his fist at the stars and asking the universe, indifferent to him as difference, to pour down its execrations upon his head.

But it is remarkable how many moral and intellectual forces in the world today converge toward another and differentiating sense in things. And there is no reason why the religious imagination cannot pass into a realistic period, accepting things-as-they-are-and-can-be, without the perpetual concern that something is missing from the picture. If there has been anything missing from the picture of things it is precisely that inner life of their own idea which is the very definition of secularity.

Among men our common logic may mean, at this moment of history, the life of the Negro and the life of man in vast undeveloped continents.

Among things the breadth of possibility is obvious. In whatever direction we look we sense an infinite to be developed or explored; the concept of the infinite in modern mathematics is a symbol for many other infinities. Here the religious imagination also hearkens back to the view of Gregory of Nyssa that human time has an infinite future for which there will be no end and that the time to explore the inner life of God is endless. There is, therefore, no need to be tormented by the image of endless time, no need to interpret religion or art as a conquest of time or of indifference, or to think of the endless vistas of the secular project as an evil. I have no doubt that all the religious images that in the Old and New Testaments seem to convey a sense of the end of time are talking not of the end of time but of the end of the processes of decay and corruption. This means that the human project will no longer have to pass through death or through all the corrupt forms of its own idea that are today causing so much unrest. In eternity there will be a less stumbling and a more moving sense of time; there will be less stuckness in the imagination.

THE DOUBLE WAY

What happened in the period of the Enlightenment was a new and major thrust of secularity into its own identity, a much more decisive thrust of the secular and the human than the Renaissance. That thrust was clouded with "fantastic" opposition to Zeus. Now we are in the presence of the greatest thrust of all, that of modernization.

The religious imagination has usually taken the view of the Renaissance in order to handle the secular crisis. That is to say, we moved along with the new forms of the secular and the human but we tried to keep them deeply fused with the forms of Christian symbolism and history. To have moved through the Renaissance world of a city like Florence was to move through an extraordinary mixture of human greatness on the one hand and the marvelous beauty of the Christic imagination on the other. Of course, this ideal fusion was in need of much mending and was already giving evidence of things coexisting that could not possibly continue to live together. Promethean figures were emerging in strength and grandeur. The glorification of man had become one of the principal themes of Renaissance literature. The lines of the human project were becoming magnificent. In Ficino and Pico the thrust of the new moment comes off with greatness but with sobriety; in Giordano Bruno we are back in the most defiant moments of Prometheus.

But the ideal of the Renaissance has *continued* as one ideal of the relationship of the sacred to the secular, a relationship of an immediate fusion of forms, histories, symbols. We have seen that any other solution has been interpreted as a disaster for the religious imagination. When our own new world did come it was interpreted as the first society of the western world not based upon religious images but based precariously upon the secular imagination, so far as it is based at all. And necessarily the religious imagination, living in this new world, was felt to be living a religious *and* a nonreligious *life*.

A Dialectical Relationship

If we are to come to a true point of unity for the religious imagination as it suffers through the divisions of sacred and secular we must decide that a common logic is important but far from sufficient. We must try to discover a dialectical relationship between sacred and secular, God and the world, that will establish not merely a common *logic*, not merely a uniting metaphor, but a common action and a common life.

The word *dialectical* here is crucial. I have already indicated how loose and flexible a word it can be. But in these pages I use it in one of its most traditional senses. I will be thinking of it as meaning *the positive and creative interplay of contraries.*

More precisely, I want to talk about the interplay, within the religious imagination, of the great contrariety of *inside* and *outside*. This imagination has begun to tackle the difficult, painful problem of secularity and to grant it autonomy and inwardness. It is at this point that the dialectical action must occur. What seems a contradiction (because we incline to think, as logical atomism did, in absolute units of thought) comes to life. This inwardness of secularity comes from the outside and is all the more inward and autonomous for doing so. It is a creation of the outside and stands in continuous relation to an outside. This means that the inwardness of secularity is a creation of God and the sacred.

We can think of outside and inside as two separate units. Then there is simple coexistence; or there may be a "confrontation"; or there may be outright hostility. We have already noted that the world, thus imaged, becomes an enemy to the interiority of man. And, thus imaged, God and the sacred become to secularity an enemy which cannot yield interiority.

The history of this image of the outside as enemy is long, tenacious, and still a powerful force among us. It has been part of that set of feelings and attitudes we have identified with Prometheanism. If we go no further back than to the figure of Giordano Bruno at the time of the Renaissance, we meet with a sharply etched example. He is a figure who claims complete interiority and is fearful that any relationship to the outside world might be the end of autonomy.

> The only passion that reigns in Bruno is the passion of the self-affirmation of the ego, heightened to titanic and heroic proportions. Although the ego recognizes that there is something transcendent, something that lies beyond human powers of conception, it nevertheless does not want to receive this super-sensible something as a simple gift of grace. The man who passively receives such a gift may perhaps possess a greater good than the man who tries to attain a knowledge of the divine through his own power; but this objective-good does not counterbalance the specific value of independent striving and action. . . . With characteristic precision, Giordano Bruno reveals the forces that press toward such a dissolution [of the bond between the idea of humanity and the idea of Christianity]. The ideal of humanity includes the ideal of autonomy; but as the ideal of autonomy becomes stronger, it dissociates itself more and more from the realm of religion—the realm into which Cusanus and the Florentine Academy had tried to force the concept of humanity.[5]

The whole understanding of autonomy and inwardness and independence now begins to take on the contours of an atomic fact that depends on nothing but itself. We have seen that in Goethe the image of the artist as Prometheus, as creative spirit living on its own resources, takes on a sharper form; it even alarms himself. But it has become a very common image of self for the artist and the writer in western culture.

These earlier images grow slowly into a creed. Philip Rieff now proposes, in his *The Triumph of the Therapeutic Man*, that we are indeed in the midst of another revolution, one in which man proposes, for his own salvation, to become purely psychological man, not only with himself as center but also cut off as much as possible from reality commitments. I do not know if this is true and am inclined to think it an exaggeration of our situation. But the mere fact that it can be seriously proposed as a hypothesis is a sign of the prevalence of the images of the outside as enemy of autonomy. If we restrict ourselves to the American scene there is evidence enough that the image is there, not in any formal guise but in the more important guise of actual attitudes and styles of life. There is a fear of dependence. There is a corresponding set of images of the outside world (the system, the establishment, the elite) which touch on real and serious defects of our society but which go beyond a *point of degree* called for by reality. These images represent real problems, but very often they are so strong that they rule out any possibility of dialogue or a final reconciliation and collaboration or any dialectical relation with the "cosmocentric" forces involved. The difference and the gap has now become not political but metaphysical.

As it deals increasingly with secularity the unique contribution of the religious imagination should move toward a reconciliation between inside and outside, between the anthropocentric and the cosmocentric. It should study this form of dialectical thought and imagination, and should be aware that it too has made many mistakes in its images of the outside.

But study is not enough. This imagination must work toward active and living solutions, even though for a time this will seem like the living of a double life. The more part of the religious imagination leads an autonomous life in the secular world, the more it must lead the life of prayer. The more it discovers the outside world, the more it must lead its own inward life. The more it does not any longer impose its own symbols or referential meanings on the world, the more it must be in touch with its own history and forms. The more it gives up Christ, the more it must find him. It is not too much to expect the final development of an easy back and forth between the two lives.

For, finally, the autonomy of the secular, the autonomy of the world, comes from the outside we call God. It is a creation of the outside, and in that sense a creation of the secular by the sacred. So much is this the case that if there were no secular world the sacred would have to create it. "I have come that you may have life and have it more abundantly." Autonomy is not a defiance but a grace.

There is still this hunger for the still fused visions of the Renaissance. But now the historical moment compels us to see that neither these visions nor any of those that preceded them is identical with Christianity. Our new moment may turn out to be the most faithful of all moments to the Christian meaning of identity, inner life, redemption, salvation, freedom, autonomy. Such a world had always been there in some degree; it had always been thought of as neutral or nonreligious; there is no reason why it cannot be imagined as the most religious of all the areas in the religious consciousness, for it is the reception of freedom from him who is free, the reception of difference and identity from the God of Abraham, Isaac, and Jacob. And how shall it avoid becoming only a beautiful humanism? By understanding how terrible a place the secular is and in what terrible need it stands.

THE SACRED: A REEMERGENCE

Now it is precisely at this point that the religious imagination comes full circle in its imagining. What is called for is a reemergence of the sacred (a reemergence of the God of Abraham, Isaac, and Jacob) in all its separateness and unique identity. But it is here that I would like to insert my modification of the position of Richard Niebuhr in *Christ and Culture*. This reemergence of the sacred does not occur in the name of the preservation of a tension between sacred and secular; that is to say, the sacred does not now reappear, in fear and dread, to be balance against secularity, to make up for the lacks, the evils, the dangers, the wasteland quality of the latter. The separate reemergence, in greater clarity than ever before, is necessary and positive, as principle of assertion of all that is most essential to the idea of secularity. The sacred, in a word, must reassert itself in its own right and refuse at all cost to be dissolved into anything other than itself. And granted the serious necessity of constant reformation and adjustment of its institutions, it is completely naïve to think that the assertion of itself should come as assertion of pure Idea and not an embodied, an institutional Idea. The counterforces it has to deal with in the secular order, the forces of evil or of passivity that run counter to a truly human order, are too powerful to be dealt with by pure Idea. They require the Son of God himself as opponent; they still require to be met by a distinct and recognizable embodiment of the rights of the sacred; Christ is prime paradigm of all redemptions.

Let me now put two apparently divergent thoughts together.

1. I agree with all those who hunger today for the discovery of a deeper and more relevant relationship of sacred and secular. I have protested against the concentration of all things good and human in the order of the sacred and the corresponding emptying of the secular order. For the two worlds have been too clearly divided and we have lived through too sharp a separation. In this whole vast everyday world where we live and breathe, buy and sell, we will often not be too sure which is which. We have decided, with passion, that it is not always necessary or good to decide.

Good then, we badly need a period of obscurity between the lines of the sacred and the secular and I hope that my own image adds to the confusion.

2. But I hold just as strongly to the separation as I do to the confusion between sacred and secular; here, regretfully, I part company from very many as we decide to move into a new historical moment. There is and must be another area, of high specificity, where the sacred, precisely as sacred, must emerge with greater clarity and identity than ever before. One reason is for its own sake, to keep declaring, as Israel did, the place of God. That having been said, we have found another reason for the absolute separation of the sacred from everything else in human civilization: the preservation of the principles of inner life and unconditionality in secularity itself.

We should explore the hypothesis that nothing short of all the identity, all the historical actuality, and all the resources of the sacred, will be required for so great a task. The situation indeed comes full circle. We began by asking the sacred to give up its own forms, in a kind of descent into hell, in order to form the first stage of a new image of secularity based on the inner unconditional life of the latter. We even asked Christ to give up many of the kingdoms the religious imagination had assigned to him. We now confront the paradox that even this first stage will finally require every resource of the sacred. Every stage of our image makes this all the more true, especially the remembrance of the terror and greatness of the secular order. To live and breathe in the modern world is no task for a disarmed imagination. It is only the Son of God who can finally prevail; what greater tribute to the secular project than this?

Moment after moment, struggle after struggle, within secular history, will require every resource of the sacred. Let me give a present example. We are engaged in a revolutionary attempt to purify much of the contemporary inhumanity of the secular project. The need is there, the intention superb. But the new movement also falls into many threatening forms of hysteria, partly the result of dreams that cannot be mastered and partly the result of those incredible rhythms of evangelical guilt in American history that are not yet mastered. It is a new form of witches' brew and devil hunt, burning with zeal and with scapegoats. Once more the project is in the tumult of a search for innocence. It will take every resource of the religious imagination to help men to say no to every form of hysteria, to every ideological group, to every package-deal way of interpreting reality. That the mind should stay free and think its own thoughts within this hysteria is no mean task.

The search for innocence is and always has been a difficult and a dangerous task. It is no criticism, it is a defense of the secular project and of human freedom, to point out that this search can be either realistic or hysterical. The discussion and revelation of the hysterical forms will make true movement in the project possible. To live without hysteria will need a very powerful spirituality.

This is part of our modern problem, as we try to move forward again in the secular project; it was surely part of the problem of Prometheus on that lonely Caucasian crag.

NOTES TO THE PROLOGUE

1. J. O. Urmson, *Philosophical Analysis* (New York: Oxford, 1956), p. 173.

2. *Prometheus Bound*, ll. 228–244. All texts from *Prometheus Bound* and the *Oresteia* are from the translations of David Grene and Richmond Lattimore, *Aeschylus I and Aeschylus II* (Chicago: Univ. of Chicago, 1953–56).

3. From the trans. by Thomas Okey, Illustrated Modern Library ed. of *The Divine Comedy* (New York: Random House, 1944), pp. 217, 220.

4. Cf. Erich Auerbach, *Mimesis: The Representation of Reality in Western Literature* (Princeton: Princeton Univ. Press, 1968), pp. 199–200.

5. Bernard Berenson, *The Italian Painters of the Renaissance* (1894–1907; rpt. London: Phaidon, 1952), p. 76.

6. Bernard Knox, *The Heroic Temper* (Berkeley: Univ. of California, 1964), p. 5.

7. Cf. also Knox's *Oedipus at Thebes* (New Haven: Yale, 1957).

8. Cedric H. Whitman, "The Matrix of Heroism: Ajax," in *The Hero in Literature*, ed. Victor Brombert (Greenwich, Conn.: Fawcett, 1969), p. 76.

9. Cf. the work of the distinguished Pirandello critic Adriano Tilgher, *Studi sul teatro contemporaneo* (Rome: Libreria di Scienze e Lettre, 1923).

10. Pirandello, *To Clothe the Naked*, trans. by William Murray (New York: Dutton, 1962), p. 75.

11. Francis Fergusson, "Oedipus Rex: The Tragic Rhythm of Action," *The Idea of a Theatre* (Garden City, N.Y.: Doubleday, 1953), pp. 25–53. Kenneth Burke, the distinguished literary critic and philosopher of the imagination, will be best discovered in *The Philosophy of Literary Form, Studies in Symbolic Action* (New York: Vintage, 1957); *A Grammar of Motives* (New York: Prentice-Hall, 1945); *A Rhetoric of Motives* (New York: Prentice-Hall, 1950); *Permanence and Change, an Anatomy of Purpose* (Los Altos: Hermes, 1954).

12. In my own theorizing about the life of the imagination I tend to eliminate the classical distinction between perception and imagination and to attribute an extraordinary and creative content to simple and basic images. For a similar logic of perception and image see John MacMurray, *The Self as Agent* (London: Faber, 1956). For a review and criticism of the fundamental statement of empiricism that there is a pure given in sensation (antecedent to all reflections and imagining) see Wilfrid Sellars, "Empiricism and the Philosophy of the Mind," in H. Feigl and M. Scriven, eds., *The Foundations of Science and The Concepts of Psychology and Psychoanalysis*, Minnesota Studies in the Philosophy of Science I (Minneapolis: Univ. of Minnesota, 1956). Still wider forms of this question are taken up by T. S. Kuhn, *The Structure of Scientific Revolutions* (Chicago: Univ. of Chicago, 1962); P. A. Feyerabend, "Explanation, Reduction and Empiricism," in H. Feigl and G. Maxwell, eds., *Scientific Explanation, Space and Time*, Minnesota Studies in the Philosophy of Science III (Minneapolis: Univ. of Minnesota,

1962); S. Korner, *Conceptual Thinking* (New York: Dover, 1955). See also Act One, note 2.

13. Graham Greene, *A Burnt-Out Case* (New York: Viking, 1961), pp. 3, 133, 245.

14. *The Comedians* (New York: Viking, 1966), p. 239.

15. P. G. Schrotenboer, *A New Apologetics: An Analysis and Appraisal of the Eristic Theology of Emil Brunner* (The Netherlands: Kok-Kampen, 1955), pp. 18–19.

16. Jacob Taubes, "On the Nature of the Theological Method: Some Reflections on the Methodological Principles of Tillich's Theology," in *Toward a New Christianity*, ed. Thomas J. J. Altizer (New York: Harcourt, 1967).

17. As I have interpreted the dialogue in *An Approach to the Metaphysics of Plato through the Parmenides* (Washington: Georgetown, 1959) the famous eight hypotheses of the second part are to be totaled up or put together into one single hypothesis or image of anything in any order that is a true unity. Each hypothesis is logically related to the others but also keeps its identity as a separate "moment" in the definition of unity. Cf. especially p. 24, note 1, and p. 25: ". . . a problem has been set early in the *Parmenides*, various hypotheses are proposed to resolve it, and the eight hypotheses are in their totality, as a unified logical system, the final successful solution to the original problem. In the technical Platonic sense, they form one single, climactic hypothesis."

NOTES TO ACT ONE
THE SEARCH FOR MAN

1. *The Republic*, trans. H. D. P. Lee (London, 1955), II, 361–362.

2. I cannot stress too strongly that the modern secular fact may be unconditional but there is nothing more unmodern than a fact without relation or context or generality. The best short analytical study I have been able to find on the subject is by Edwin B. Allaire, "Bare Particulars," in *Essays in Ontology*, Iowa Publications in Philosophy I (Iowa City: Univ. of Iowa, 1963), pp. 14–21. This article is excellent for its treatment of the key ideas of the dependence and independence of facts. It is also a fine critique of nominalism. Rudolf Carnap, "The Old and the New Logic," in *Logical Positivism*, ed. A. J. Ayer (Glencoe, Ill.: Free Press, 1959), pp. 133 ff., is a short but careful analysis of the differences between classical and modern or relational logic. In Ernst Cassirer's *The Problem of Knowledge* (New Haven: Yale, 1950), cf. especially Chap. V, "The Goal and Methods of Theoretical Physics," pp. 110–117, for his attack on the possibility of a brute fact that does not exist within a principle or a context; Gilbert Ryle's article, "The Theory of Meaning," in *British Philosophy in the Mid-Century*, ed. C. A. Mace (New York: Macmillan, 1957), pp. 239–264, is a vigorous defense of meaning as connotation. Denotation is only one of endless forms of meaning. Compare with Cassirer

and Susanne K. Langer, *Philosophy in a New Key* (Cambridge, Mass.: Harvard, 1951).

Every nominalistic mode of thought seems to me to be the complete reverse of these contextual and relational modes. Ernest A. Moody's *The Logic of William of Ockham* (1935; rpt. New York: Russell, 1965), remains a noteworthy book on Ockham and nominalism. Georges de Lagarde, *La Naissance de l'esprit laïque au déclin du moyen age*, Vol. V, *L'Individualisme Ockamiste* (Paris: Librairie Droz, 1946), contains a study of nominalism and the metaphysics of the individual. I note especially the way in which Ockham uses the word *absolute* to describe a thing; with him the word means its radical independence of everything surrounding it. Something can be a unity of many things, but even then it is for him a unity of many absolutes. Another way in which he describes an existant is by the quality of insularity and the ability to be completely circumscribed. Lagarde is correct when he says that all this is not modern.

3. Norman Cohn, *The Pursuit of the Millennium* (New York: Harper, 1961), pp. 307–308.

4. Ibid., p. 315.

5. Two learned studies of the infinite in modern thought are: C. F. Weizsäcker, *The World View of Physics* (London: Routledge, 1952), which includes a study of the infinite in modern physics. It also takes the strong position that part of our intellectual crisis is rooted in our abandonment of the symbol. Cf. pp. 155 circa. Alexandre Koyré, *From the Closed World to the Infinite Universe* (Baltimore: Johns Hopkins, 1957), which is a study of the history of the infinite in modern thought, beginning with Nicholas of Cusa.

6. Frank Kermode, *Continuities* (London: Routledge and Kegan Paul, 1968), p. 75.

7. For the sake of the continuity of my argument between a previous book [*Images of Hope* (Baltimore: Helicon, 1964)] and this present work—both are searching for images of unconditionality—I will take the liberty of citing several passages from the former: "It is something of this order that an ideal relationship [such as love or friendship] does to a wish. Ideally it will denude it or defuse it of everything but itself. It will help it or allow it to emerge as exactly what it is. What will it mean when I say that I want a cup of coffee? Under the influence of a good relationship it will mean exactly that and nothing more. It will not engulf the wish in a situation that raises questions about it. It will not suggest that it is a sign or symbol of anything else, whether of hostility or love. Certainly it will not create an aura of hostility around it. But even more important, it will not make it a sign or a condition of love. ('I approve of your taking coffee. I like coffee, too. It is a sign that you love me. I love you.') The freedom to take coffee may be created by a good relationship, but if it is an ideal wish it cannot itself create the relationship or be a condition for it. Such a wish must be unconditioned. It is created by the outside world but it is not conditioned by it. Therefore every real wish, no matter how small, is a truly creative act, introducing a brand new thing into the world.

"Such a wish and such an act is a far cry from the wish and act of the romantic rebel. It is more involved in reality, in relationship, and in the imagination which imagines the real. But it is just as free, autonomous and unconditioned as any romantic wish would ever hope to be" (pp. 155–156).

"This is the most extraordinary and most fruitful form of mutuality in the world. Granted our presence to reality and to love, God wishes us to choose, in the knowledge that it is all right to choose and that choosing and wishing make the choice all right. This is not subjectivity or solipsism because every choice of love is related to reality and is the choice of a reality. On the other hand, neither is it magic—which would be the case if there were only one choice among thousands which would be the best, and God help us if we do not find it. The theological supposition that there is one right way is the ultimate source of all externalism.

"This kind of 'magic' has the effect and intention of absolving us from wishing and thinking, and from all the operations of a truly interior life. It supposes that there is some one precise, magical thing or person or event in the world outside us that will happily come along to do the wishing for us. It allows us to project our identity, our capacity for thinking and feeling and wishing, outside ourselves, and so we are left haunted by that sense of a lack of identity characteristic of all our illnesses.

"There are other ghosts to haunt and afflict us. If we insist upon inserting 'morality' into the wrong places, if we insist that there is one right answer for everything, if we require that the object do all the wishing, without the mutuality of our own wishing, there are ghastly consequences. First of all, the process never works; it introduces an endless and exhausting search into life. Pure externalism involves endlessness. Secondly, no matter what we do within such terms as these, there is a sense of failure and of guilt and of being judged by some anonymous object with which, no matter what we do, we cannot make contact. For this magical object we seek, this one right thing, is really nonexistent; but it exercises a strange and absolute tyranny over everything we do. Because we are not free and because we lack Christian interiority, we are oppressed by an anonymous and ruthless sense of law. The strange myths of the novels of Franz Kafka are full of this sense of constant and anonymous judgment upon ourselves from which we have no recourse, for the guilt cannot be located, and the judge is anonymous, and the judgment without reason. How can such a psychology or theology produce anything but hopelessness?" (pp. 173–174).

8. Carl Michalson, *Worldy Theology, The Hermeneutical Forms of an Historical Faith* (New York: Scribner, 1967).

9. William O. Fennell, "The Theology of True Secularity," in *New Theology No. 2*, ed. M. E. Marty and D. G. Peerman (New York: Macmillan, 1965), pp. 29–30.

10. Ronald Gregor Smith, *The New Man* (New York: Harper, 1956); *Secular Christianity* (New York: Harper, 1966).

1. The following from *The New Man* is an overly rhetorical version of a

not unusual claim to the separation of modern history from metaphysical and medieval blocks:

"The change was in man's self-understanding. That is to say, the change lay within his understanding of history. History was no longer seen as the necessary but tiresome ante-chamber of supra-history, but as an existent power whose meaning could be sought in itself. This was the fundamental insight which broke the bonds of mediaeval metaphysics, and with it the very structure of mediaeval civilization. Out of this has flowed the work of the natural sciences from Francis Bacon to Heisenberg, of literature from Shakespeare to Mr. Eliot, of historical criticism from Lessing to Bultmann, of modern philosophy from Giordano Bruno to the philosophers of linguistic analysis, of political science from Machiavelli to Lenin—and indeed of every sphere over which human activity has ranged and flowered in the last five hundred years. All this activity was possible because man understood his situation in history in a new way. He saw himself as free, and as responsible for making his own life, and as open to a future which was not an arbitrary or threatening disposition of fate, but was awaiting him as his own destiny. History came to be seen as the way in which man understood his own being as the free and responsible climax to his given situation" (pp. 40–41).

The difficulty with this kind of statement is that it forgets how profoundly ahistorical so much of the history of secularization has been. Despite every tribute we can pay to the genius of the Enlightenment, it seems not to have possessed any historical genius or sense. R. G. Collingwood in The Idea of History (New York: Oxford, 1946), puts the problem thus: ". . . the historiography of the Enlightenment is apocalyptic to an extreme degree, as indeed the very word 'enlightenment' suggests. The central point of history, for these writers, is the sunrise of the modern scientific spirit. Before that, everything was superstition and darkness, error and imposture. And of these things there can be no history, not only because they are unworthy of historical study, but because there is in them no rational or necessary development: the story of them is a tale told by an idiot, full of sound and fury, signifying nothing.

"Thus in the crucial case, namely the origin of the modern scientific spirit, these writers could have no conception of historical origins or processes. Pure reason cannot come into existence out of pure unreason. There can be no development leading from the one to the other. The sunrise of the scientific spirit was, from the point of view of the Enlightenment, a sheer miracle, unprepared in the previous course of events and uncaused by any cause that could be adequate to such an effect. This inability to explain or expound historically what they regarded as the most important event in history was of course symptomatic; it meant that in a general way they had no satisfactory theory of historical causation and could not seriously believe in the origin or genesis of anything whatever" (pp. 79–80).

For an analysis of the static and nonhistorical quality of the image of man in the Enlightenment see Lucien Goldmann, L'Illuminismo e la società moderna (Turin, 1967), p. 48 and circa.

It would seem that a fundamental weakness in the attempts of the Enlightenment to be historical was the rebirth within it of a constantly recurring pseudo-Platonism. There is a natural and ideal order of perfection and an actual order which is always a corrupt failure to reach the ideal. This is also the weakness of much modern dialectical thought, which is one of the successors of the Enlightenment. There is no history. There are only perfection and corruption. I know it is easy to say it but it is necessary to say that an important crux for us must always be the work of equating time and idea, fact and value. The ways in which this can be said (and done) are endless. But I have just been reading an article by the Lutheran theologian Jaroslav Pelikan [*Crosscurrents* XIX (1969), No. 4, pp. 375–384] in which he cites the following sentence from Whitehead in *Adventure of Ideas:* "I hazard the prophecy that that religion will conquer which can render clear to popular understanding some eternal greatness incarnate in the passage of temporal fact." I share Dr. Pelikan's approval of that sentence.

12. For a concentrated version of his position see Friedrich Gogarten, *The Reality of Faith* (Philadelphia: Westminster, 1959), especially Chapter 13, "A New Understanding of Faith," pp. 105–111. See Larry Shiner, *The Secularization of History: An Introduction to the Theology of Friedrich Gogarten* (Nashville: Abingdon, 1966).

13. Schubert M. Ogden, *The Reality of God* (New York: Harper, 1966).

14. "Whether there is, as Gogarten argues, some causal relationship between Protestantism and the autonomy of the sciences is a question we may leave for the historians of ideas to decide. The point is that the dialectical theologians believed that the virtues of autonomy and intellectual responsibility are related in an intimate fashion to faith, when faith is understood not as belief in doctrine but as trust in being itself." Van Austin Harvey, *The Historian and the Believer* (New York: Macmillan, 1966), p. 136.

15. Norman Cohn, *The Pursuit of the Millennium*, gives us some fascinating materials on the manner in which the Brethren of the Free Spirit and similar groups were able to co-relate intense degrees of absolute innocence and absolute indictments of the least appearance of evil in others.

16. Jacques Ellul, *The Technological Society* (New York: Knopf, 1965), p. xxv.

17. Quoted in C. Kerényi, *Prometheus: Archetypal Image of Human Existence*, trans. Ralph Manheim, Bollingen Series XLV (New York: Pantheon, 1963), p. 6.

18. Raymond Trousson, *Le Thème de Prométhée dans la littérature Européenne*, 2 vols. (Geneva: Librairie Droz, 1964).

19. Werner Jaeger, *Paideia, The Ideals of Greek Culture*, trans. Gilbert Highet, 3 vols. (New York: Oxford, 1939–44), I, 260.

20. *Prometheus Bound*, ll. 1–51.

21. William Y. Tindall, *Samuel Beckett* (New York: Columbia, 1964), p. 26.

22. *Christ and Apollo* (New York: Sheed & Ward, 1960), p. 176.

NOTES TO ACT TWO
THE SEARCH FOR LIGHT

1. The relation between neurosis and the rigidity of our images has been explored in a substantive way by the distinguished psychoanalytical writer Lawrence S. Kubie. His major work should be read for the psychoanalytic version of the trap. Cf. *Practical and Theoretical Aspects of Psychoanalysis*, (New York: International Universities Press, 1950); "The Fundamental Nature of the Distinction between Normality and Neurosis," in *The Psychoanalytic Quarterly* XXIII (1954), 167–204. In *Neurotic Distortions of the Creative Process* (Lawrence, Kans.: Univ. of Kansas, 1958), Kubie attacks the traditional association of neurosis with the creative imagination. Neurosis is a state of rigidity and trappedness; the truly creative artist is free.

2. Hermann Diels and Walther Kranz, *Die Fragmente der Vorsokratiker* (Berlin, 1934), p. 172, frag. 94 (from Plutarch, *de exil.*, II, 604A).

3. For a study of the idea of development in the God of Aeschylus see Friedrich Solmsen, *Hesiod and Aeschylus* (Ithaca: Cornell, 1949).

4. *The Libation Bearers*, ll. 268–296.

5. J. O. Urmson, *Philosophical Analysis* (New York: Oxford, 1956), p. 173.

6. Gustave Glotz, *Histoire grecque* (Paris: Les presses universitaires de France, 1929), I, 430.

7. *The Eumenides*, ll. 1044–1047.

8. Later published in *The American Scholar*, Spring, 1966, pp. 233–242.

NOTES TO ACT THREE
THE SEARCH FOR INNOCENCE

1. C. E. Black, *The Dynamics of Modernization* (New York: Harper, 1966), p. 2 (the final chapter of this book takes the form of a very useful critical bibliography on modernization).

2. *Prometheus Bound*, ll. 441–442.

3. Black, p. 4.

4. Ibid., p. 7.

5. Ibid., p. 27.

6. Raymond Aron, *Progress and Disillusion, The Dialectics of Modern Society* (New York: Praeger, 1968), p. 128.

7. Cited by C. Kerényi in his *Prometheus: Archetypal Image of Human Existence*, trans. Ralph Manheim, Bollingen Series XLV (New York: Pantheon, 1963), pp. 4–6.

8. Cf. Lionel Trilling, *Beyond Culture* (New York: Viking, 1955), pp. 57–87, and *The Liberal Imagination* (New York: Viking, 1952).

9. See *New York Times*, Feb. 25, 1970.

10. For documentation see *New York Times*, Mar. 9, 1970.

11. Loren Eiseley, *The Unexpected Universe* (New York: Harcourt, 1969), pp. 38–39.

12. Ibid., p. 36.

13. Ibid., pp. 37–44.

14. Karl Popper, *The Open Society and Its Enemies*, 3rd rev. ed (London: Routledge and Kegan Paul, 1957), pp. 278–279.

NOTES TO THE EPILOGUE

1. Rudolf Otto, *The Idea of the Holy*, trans. John W. Harvey, 2nd ed. (New York: Oxford, 1958), p. 77.

2. Job 39:13-18 as quoted by Otto, p. 79.

3. Otto, p. 80.

4. I have been helped by a fine article on the subject by Leonard J. Fein, former assistant director of Harvard-MIT Joint Center for Urban Studies, "The Limits of Liberalism," *Saturday Review*, June 20, 1970, pp. 83–85, 95–96.

5. Ernst Cassirer, *The Individual and the Cosmos in Renaissance Philosophy*, trans. Mario Domandi: (New York: Harper, 1964), pp. 97–98.

Index